HOLY DAYS AND HOLIDAYS

HOLY DAYS
AND
HOLIDAYS

Blessed Occasions for Heart and Mind

George Bendall

 DEVORSS *Publications*

ISBN: 0-87516-686-5

Library of Congress Catalog Card Number: 95-83031

DeVorss & Company, *Publisher*
Box 550
Marina del Rey, CA 90294

Contents

A Word from the Author's Wife

To fully appreciate these "holiday" talks it is necessary to understand Dr. Bendall's wholehearted devotion to God, country and home—in that order.

He prepared at great length for each holiday and would be totally immersed in the spirit of the day. Christmas and the Christmas Eve Candlelight services were devoted to love and peace. He chose the music accordingly, for the music was an integral part of the service. The sanctuary decorations were also very carefully planned.

All during the Lenten period he prepared for Easter. Fasting, he taught, concerned our spoken word and thoughts, not food or drink. In other words, it is what comes out of the mouth that counts —not what goes into it. On Good Friday his talk on the Seven Last Words was an emotional and deeply felt service.

Then there were the Patriotic Holidays, paying homage to our leaders who, at great sacrifice to themselves, gave birth to this great nation which he loved so dearly: Independence Day, Presidents Day, Veterans Day—days of extreme respect, loyalty, and love for this wonderful country we live in. And what better way to express this than with anthems sung loud and clear, such as "God Bless America," "America the Beautiful," and the "Battle Hymn of the Republic." I can still hear him saying to the congregation, "Let's bring the rafters down! This is your country, and a great one it is!"

And lest I forget the sentimental, softer side of Dr. Bendall, for he had a very gentle, caring aspect, when an occasional tear or two would fall (always in private, within his own home): there were Fathers Day and Mothers Day. Regrettably, Mothers Day tapes and notes have been lost. But those who were fortunate enough to attend one of his Mothers Day services will recall the red rosebud or the pink carnation he loved to present to each mother and how he would lovingly, with a big hug, present a corsage to the Mother of the Year he had selected for this honor. It was a beautiful day, and everyone left a little bit wiser, more loving, and a lot happier. This would be one of the Sundays he would glow, and his softness would break through the outer, more formal persona. Another would, of course, be Fathers Day, and for this, fortunately, a talk survives.

Enjoy the book—and may holidays always find you with joys to share, friends to love and memories to hold close in your heart as you move forward in God's love under His protection and direction.

ANN BENDALL

HOLY DAYS AND HOLIDAYS

A Fresh Start
NEW YEAR'S DAY

I ALWAYS LOOK FORWARD to January, especially ever since Ernest Holmes, who founded our teaching, said to me, "George, we as teachers have a habit of getting all caught up during the course of the year, and by year's end we begin to think we're advanced souls when in fact we may be forgetting the principles." So January is a good time to bring everybody back to the basic principles—because principles will never let you down. In fact, Dr. Holmes used to say to me, "People will let you down, and I may let you down, but the principles I teach you will never let you down; and if you do get let down, then you weren't listening when I taught you." Think about that.

January is named for the Roman god Janus, a two-faced god shown on coins with one face looking back, as though through the past year, and the other looking forward, as though to the New Year. So at the beginning of the New Year we stand at one of those divisions in time which we have established for our own convenience. God is timeless, but we need time so that we can measure the distance between experiences. So when the clock strikes twelve, we put away all of last year and look forward to the new one.

The division is, of course, imaginary and arbitrary. January 1st is no more the beginning of a new year than yesterday or the day before. Yet even though it's only an illusory pause, it gives us time to think, to see what we might have learned from the past year and to establish ourself in a pattern of growth. There is a line, I think from Joshua, "You have not passed this way before." And I think too of the Israelites who were about to cross the river and enter the Promised Land, because there's a parallel there between the ancient Israelites and ourselves: there's an unknown wilderness in front of us. We generally fear what is unknown—and we don't know what the New Year will bring. But we *can* know, through the faith and belief of our teaching. And the recognition of the living, loving Presence of God, and our unity with God and each other, can emerge very well through it all.

On the island of Borneo they may have an answer

to our New Year situation: each year the people get together in festive mood and build a ship that will sail out to sea—but it is a strange ship that carries no human being. In the hull and on the deck they heap a cargo of useless and worn-out articles symbolizing the evils of the past year. (A good time to clean out the closet!) The sails and rudder are set so that the ship is carried out to sea, only to be sunk in oblivion by the first storm. This sinks all the unpleasantness of the past. See how simply it very quickly erases what that past might have been! It sinks the limitations, the bondages, the mistakes, the sicknesses. Then the new year is begun fresh.

So I look at New Year's as a place where we make a fresh start. Now you and I of course know that any day can be a New Year's Day where we begin a fresh start, where we can discover that the thing we know to be always present, but have never quite gotten a grasp of, can lift us above. I wrote down a little ad from a finance company that reads: "Now you can borrow enough money to get completely out of debt." I love it. Instead, we are learning to appropriate the good that has found us—not borrow it.

In starting afresh, let's not be like the college student who wanted to create an ideal atmosphere for learning. He bought a special adjustable reading lamp and he set it next to a comfortable contoured armchair. Then he installed a revolving bookcase with special reading stand that correctly positioned the book. Next he purchased a comfortable robe and slippers—and he even burned a little pine incense to stimulate his senses. Finally, when everything was in readiness for the business of learning, he sat down in his contoured chair robed and slippered, with special light and incense, opened his book—*and promptly went to sleep*. So let's get started—but let's allow the comfort to follow. So first a willingness to give up old ideas and make room for the new one.

We need a deep and patient conviction for our fresh start. The launching of a ship is always a gala event with flags, bands, bunting and cheering crowds. In this atmosphere the ship starts out on its journey. But before it reaches port it will encounter long, drawn-out storms, howling winters, weather, and seas that make the heart stand still. This is the test of each one of us, and that is why we must work for the extra strength that will carry us. The time for calm will be when we're in port.

But you're saying, "I had a lot of *good* things take place last year." And now you come to the end of a year, you might be thinking that you don't know exactly how much of all of that old stuff you really want to get rid of. How much shall be left behind? If it's money, ring in more of the same! Yet even that isn't easy, because of the conditioning we undergo in the world in which we live. So you sit there and say, "I've heard all these words before. *If only I could change!*" You may even sit down and make an entire stack of resolutions for the New Year. I personally make *promises* to myself—because if I make a resolution, I usually seek to find a way to break it.

We may have set up false gods in the past year—the gods of effects, of structure, of organization, of building, of form. We may have set up a false god of self-pity or a false god of self-punishment. (A lot of people love to sentence themselves to punishments of mind and emotion and body that no judge would ever impose on them.) We may even have set up a false god of sickness, worshiping it and saying, "This is my condition." This is all fear—and what we fear most comes upon us, because every fear becomes a wish, and a wish is a prayer. All this then feeds the fear of what the coming year is going to bring.

Our work is a sort of counseling together. There

are no gurus; we are all learning. I'm learning from you, you're learning from some of the things I've learned from Dr. Holmes. And so our work consists in understanding the universal principles and the techniques for applyling them so that they will work in our life. We have no cut-and-dried formula. Each must establish his or her own. This is why Religious Science is known as a teaching and practicing tradition. We teach it and we endeavor to practice it. We're not too self-important to admit that we still need to learn—and perhaps to unlearn much of what we have learned in life. *The New Year is a year to learn something new—and to unlearn some of the mistakes we might have established in our last year.*

We get so confused and sometimes the words that come from any pulpit or lectern seem kind of hollow —reminding me of the bank president who gave a technical talk on the monetary system before a civic club. The talk dealt with such things as the transfer of liability, the assets, the Treasury Department, the Federal Reserve System, the commercial banks, the discount rates, the balance of payments and so forth. When he was finished he was approached by a member of the audience who said he was a minister. He said, ''That was a fine talk you gave, but frankly, I didn't understand a word of it.'' The banker replied, ''In that case, I can only tell you what you tell your listeners: have faith.''

Our work rather is a matter of permitting, call it a Divine Power—a Power of love, compassion and guidance—to work through us. Religious Science as practiced recognizes a Divine Presence, oneness with God and the healing power of pure love. It recognizes that most of us have a great deal to learn about the laws of life and even more about ourselves.

Whatever the mistakes of the past year, surrender them and let them go. And when you do, you may feel a little empty. You may feel like you've lost a good friend. But think of it: it's the new things that are the exciting things. New things are the things that keep us involved with life. Use January first as the reminder that we've outgrown all of the thinking of the past year. It is time, not fearfully but enthusiastically, to declare that it's a New Year, a new time, a new opportunity, a new feeling and a new life.

How new? As new as you want to make it. As new as the new ideas you have. As new as the new opportunity to exercise the most precious gift of all: the gift of choice. A new opportunity to demonstrate the answered prayer. A new opportunity to indulge more self-consideration. A new goal to attain and a new opportunity to appreciate the gift of life.

Consider, finally, these lines from an anonymously written poem:

> The flower unblown, a book unread,
> A tree with fruit unharvested,
> A path untrod, a house whose rooms
> Lack yet the hearts that God perfumes,
> A landscape whose wide border lies
> In silent shade beneath the skies,
> A wondrous fountain yet unsealed,
> A basket with its gifts concealed.
> This is the year that for you waits
> Beyond tomorrow's mystic gates.

A Light to Live By
PRESIDENTS DAY

THE TWO PRESIDENTS we commemorate and celebrate—Washington and Lincoln—both came to the presidency in times of confusion and turmoil. They both had to fight uphill battles to found and refound the nation, to establish and reestablish a unity. And they gave every succeeding president that same light to live by. The unity I'm referring to is not some effect that we put on like a dress or a suit of clothes. It's got to be a part of something deep within the individual, something of God awakened deep within—of the vibration and rhythm of all Nature—of a kinship, a totally unanimous feeling-together—serving a cause, dedicating oneself to that cause, putting aside selfish personal interests and just committing to that cause. It couldn't be any other way. The light to live by always gives us the opportunity to redirect our thinking or to change that thinking so that the intuitive sense within is released. That's what we dedicate ourselves to.

Each member of a nation has a mental atmosphere. The nation in turn reflects the total collective atmosphere of all of its states and all of its citizens. Individually, you and I have a mental atmosphere that reflects the total collection of our individual thinking—an atmosphere that has evolved from all we've studied, all we've thought, all we've consciously and unconsciously perceived, and all we've said and done.

It is a very real thing. At a small wedding at which I officiated recently you could just feel it. The young people outside commented on the good feeling and vibration coming from within the chapel. This is an example of the collective light—the light to live by. It is the result of a lot of meditation. It is also the result of much dedication to a common purpose. We've entered a home and we've felt the same thing that we feel in a chapel. We've felt in our bones the vibration of the store if the salesclerk was good. We've felt the vibration of the country, good or bad.

You meet someone and suddenly bells ring because you are on the same intuitive wavelength. And then you wonder whether that is normal. Or is it strange . . . weird . . . ESP—? Should you trust those feelings or shun them? The light to live by was wherever those feelings were. We should immerse ourselves in them and trust them.

It's always interesting to me that with a group of people you can change one attitude and all the other attitudes will change. I can actually observe the changes from Sunday to Sunday. These deep-rooted feelings reflect on the long-term welfare of the group and on the long-term welfare of our own individual lives. Opportunities for growth and for personal achievement open up. In fact, we get opportunities to jump at. (I told someone that you need to jump at the opportunities you are offered. He asked how you knew when to jump. I said you don't; you just have to keep on jumping.)

Washington and Lincoln knew that we're no better nor worse than others. They knew that we were a unique breed of people. We didn't seek favors and we weren't granted favors. They knew we had to be welded together in an established order of operation. They knew that there were many varied thoughts, beliefs, attitudes and feelings in the body politic. They didn't believe that God thought America was a special place. The light they wanted to establish was that God existed within the heart of every citizen and within every state and guided all of its action. Now we study and we work together to make what we call a spiritual demonstration. We pray, and a result takes place. In the same way, the founders of this nation wanted a demonstration of the pursuit of happiness and joy as part of their conviction in the founding of the nation.

Every time we are successful in demonstration we say Thank God for our teaching and for our belief. And we understand that if our prayers are not successful, if so-called healing demonstrations don't seem to take place in our life, it's not because God's law is at fault. Rather, we are clinging to some old ideas, or a cluster of ideas, that have acted as a barrier. Washington faced this problem of old ideas and clusters of ideas and he had to bring them all into line in one Union from thirteen colonies. Lincoln too knew that it had to be done even though we had to engage in a war that has had more casualties than any other war since—the War between the States—to accomplish that. We believe, and it was established, that this should be a country of abundance with no one dwelling in fear or lack. In this we largely triumphed. We are facing similar conditions in this country today, and we are bringing about changes as fast as we can.

Now many of us have made small demonstrations of prayer with ease. You've gone to the supermarket and told yourself that you knew you could find a parking place, and you demonstrated it. You told yourself you knew you could find the right car, and you demonstrated it. You said you knew you could find the right teaching, and you demonstrated that too—because you're here with us. You've demonstrated in this way with ease and dispatch.

But somewhere there may be some great prayer unanswered, and for some reason it's not taking place—that great healing of mind or body or spirit that we seek, or the harmonizing of our lives. Perhaps it was in part the spirit of the early presidents of this great nation who inspired Ralph Waldo Emerson to say, "There is no great and there is no small to the soul that maketh all, and where it cometh all things are; and it comes everywhere." Only on the human side of you and me is there great and small, important and trivial, easy and difficult. Within the Mind of God, and in the Idea of God, there is no small, trivial, difficult. There is no impossible. There is no unanswerable question, no unsolvable problem, no situation not subject to the healing harmony of God.

If you desire to make that master demonstration, keep in mind Dr. Ernest Holmes' teaching—but remember that all of the truly great leaders of the world practice what we study without putting a label on it. And I'm sure Washington and Lincoln thought in this same way. But we can't demonstrate abundance and remain immersed in thoughts of lack and limitation. Be like the farmer, pail in hand, who looked at his cow and said, "Well, Bossy, what will it be: milk or hamburger?" Similarly, you can't demonstrate physical healing while centering your attention on symptoms and painful conditions. The more symptoms you worship, the more they become affixed to you.

In our teaching we believe that we have the ability to find healing in the physical body and in the body of our affairs when we are willing to face the reality of some of the uncomfortable facts and then proceed to the beautiful truth. When it's more *real* for us to know the truth, that's when we shall *really* know it. When it's more real to us to know that God is in our life, that's when we'll have the ability to select and animate and enjoy life for what it was meant to be.

We as free Americans have the ability to feel intuitively. There is no repression to our feelings; we are permitted to feel all—within the framework of good order. As individuals, we have that intuitive sense. An intuitive use of God's power will gradually awaken a recognition of your inner self—and suddenly it's there. *The power is there.* We have choosing-power as "standard equipment." We can choose whatever we wish. The first president of this country and Abraham Lincoln wanted that right of choice to be given to a vast collection of individuals. Such was the light that they themselves lived by.

So as we feel loving thoughts, as we have an atmosphere of caring and a goal, as we feel a certain amount of pride and success, we *affirm* it, *expect* it—and then we begin to find that that is the truth about ourselves. That's when it's great—when suddenly we can say, "Why was I swimming against the stream?" Catherine Ponder says in one of her books, "There's gold dust in the air"—and indeed there is: the gold dust of freedom, of unity, of dedication to a purpose. This is the wealth that established a Nation united under one set of laws organized for the benefit of society.

The Bible says God isn't mocked and some others —practicing metaphysicians—say we can't fool the law. The light to live by is precisely this great truth. Jesus taught that it is done to me as I believe, because my true, deep-down, honest-to-God beliefs are always revealed. They really never remain hidden. My true beliefs determine my life; and I have control over my true beliefs. The light to live by, the light that is within each one of us no matter how we happen to thnk of it, may always be fanned anew into expression. We may cover it, but we can never put it out. When we let that light shine forth, then we fulfill the saying, "Your light shall shine before you." And that's the light to live by. The light of what America stood for shone forth. Though a relatively new country in the gazetteers of the world, we have given all other nations a light to live by.

And so we pray. We pray by thinking. We pray by feeling. We pray by organized prayer, or treatment; but however we do it, we see that God is in and through all.

For what is prayer but the expansion of yourself into the living ether? . . .

And if you cannot but weep when your soul summons you to prayer, she should spur you again and yet again, though weeping, until you shall come laughing.

—Kahlil Gibran

In other words, it's not something we have to work for, but something we permit to take place: the light making itself visible by our own choice, guiding us and touching every part of our body and our being—a light that stands for definite principles of unity beginning with belief in God, belief in this community, belief in this state and this nation. And that light is the same light "that lighteth the world," and a light that all others can feel in the same way.

In Love with—Love!
VALENTINE'S DAY

VALENTINE'S DAY—or, as we used to call it, *Saint* Valentine's Day—was established a long time ago; and did you know it has absolutely no relation to the saint? It goes back to an old custom—in the Norman language, *gallantine*, meaning "lover," and pronounced as *Valentine*, the name of the saint. The old custom was for a young girl to boil an egg, extract the yolk, fill the cavity with salt and then eat the whole before going to bed. This made her dream, and she'd see her future husband.

Valentine's Day: hearts, flowers and candy, love. We talk about love not as a weak, soporific kind of emotion, but as something strong that shares, that sustains, cares, and allows for growth, fulfilling Paul's statement "God is Love." For this is the way we look at God, allowing us to grow—a love that binds together, brings together and holds together. I have often thought: if you could take away love for one second, what would happen to this world we live in?

I find that most people are in love with—love! The idea of it is tremendous; and since God is the highest absolute Value, then love is *God's* highest value; for infinite love *is* God. It has no limits. It is always there. And yet it's impossible to define what it is. We can use dictionary definitions or synonyms, but each individual must feel it for him- or herself. We can say this: it is something that can be absorbed, assumed, distributed—a kind of glowing feeling that takes place; something that is unconditional and that lasts forever.

There comes to mind the story of the young man who was proposing to the reluctant girl. He said to her, "You know I really love you. I'd climb the highest mountain, I'd swim the deepest river, I'd go through the fiercest jungle—for you."

She asked, "Would you *die* for me?"

He replied, "No; my love is an *undying* love."

I think the question always remains whether we don't seek it rather than have it, and have it rather than give it. But Valentine's Day is that day where we give it of ourselves.

And we give it in many ways. I talk to a lot of

people and I find that in most of our lives the idea of giving love is scarce. We want it, we need it—because everyone must be loved. But we almost say to ourselves, "I cannot afford to love for fear I'll be vulnerable." We say, "I'm too old to learn what it is all about"—yet we know that science says *you're never too old*. We even say, "I've never been good-looking, so how can love come to me?" Of course, we in our teaching know that beauty is the externalization of the harmony within.

So we put limiting obstacles in the way, and, being hard on ourselves, we forget that we have a Silent Partner as well as a physical partner and that the Silent Partner is always there giving to us. Now think for a moment of the beautiful precision with which Nature functions. There really isn't much strife in Nature. The bulbs know when it is time to stick their shoots up above ground. They have that clockwork that tells them when winter is over. They always seem to operate without a problem in perfect order.

But *we* continue to think that *we're* different, that God has done something different to us. In our teaching we talk about God as an Infinite Thinker, an Intelligence in and through all things, a Mind which knows all, if you will—the Mind of God. But, we also say that it acts in a field which provides all. That's perfect love. It brings everything together at the right time in the right way and shares everything it has, thus maintaining our world as a unity.

It's the same when two people decide to spend their life together and get married. It is not what they are going to *get* from each other; it's what they have to *give* to each other, and this brings them together in one unit. So it's a sweet, beautiful thing—but not a sentimental thing. There's something impersonal, yet very personal, about it which promotes and organizes and brings to pass and maintains the structure of our own personal desires. It always seems to work out that way.

I also think that, in order to give, we have to think about how to give to ourselves. It's so easy sometimes to give to others; but do we give to ourselves? We miss so much by not being good to ourselves, like the employee whose boss scowled at him when he came in late and said, "You should have been here at nine!" The employee said, "Why? What happened at nine?"

The greatest thing is to give ourselves all the necessary elements that strengthen us and allow us fearlessly to give of ourselves in all areas. Even though it may appear to be selfish, it's not. Can you look at yourself and say, "I love myself because I am a living, loving expression of God"? Can you say, "I like myself because of what I am, despite what I'm not"? The truth of the matter is we are all of one nature. We all have different bodies, faces and forms; but, deep within us we laugh together, we cry together, we love together—regardless of the language or color or creed. And this always produces some generating action within.

One thing I have found out: no man, no woman or child can live without love. It is impossible. The great teachers, the great practitioners of spiritual mind-healing, the great doctors, the great therapists may have all the technical knowlege in the world. But if the individual doesn't feel the love it's all for naught.

Love is that factor that constitutes the healing element. It's an extension of ourselves, so that it takes a form. We say to someone, "I love you," not just to say *I love you*; inside, we are saying *I care what happens to you, I understand.* Yet sometimes we talk of love in an offhand way. We say, "Oh, isn't that wonderful! God is Love!" and then ignore some people because we *also* say *we can't love them*. I always excused myself with "I love everybody—but there's a lot of people I don't like," and I thought that let me off the hook.

Then I went to work and prayed for myself. Somehow it reminded me of the real-estate agent who said, "I'll try once again" and showed an old house to a woman who, when she looked at it, said, "I could do a lot with that"; but then, after a moment's thought, she added: "however that's what I said when I first saw my husband." Love is positive when men and women love each other not just for self-gratification but love each other because they have something to give—a swapping of strengths and weaknesses. It's positive when we know a child shall grow into manhood or womanhood with these ideas. It's positive when we give everything in our life to make our family happy.

I have always felt that the great leaders of the Nation—Washington, Lincoln, the great religious figures and other greats of our country—directed their love and emotional nature to the cause that they believed in: the Union of these United States. I have always felt that an artist gives her love to what she portrays on canvas because she steps back from the canvas and sees not the object she looked at but what her loving emotions within her revealed to her. So in essence the painting is a painting of the feeling within.

I have always felt that musicians must have that love. There are many musicians who technically can play and pound out the notes—but there has to be an invisible essence of loving harmony. This is present when there is nonresistance and self-surrender— one of the most difficult things in the world. Jesus, Mahatma Gandhi, the Buddha were all proponents of nonresistance, because they recognized that whatever you resist you have given power to, and then it resists you. So they loved unconditionally—a form of self-surrender. The Bible tells us when we pray to believe we already have, and so we say, "Thank you, God," accepting that we already have it. Ask and you shall receive. *In His name* means *in His nature*, and so we talk about love, the very creative Principle.

The plants, the earth and the sun—there is a love that reveals itself in these things, a creative principle that we use. We take an idea in our mind and we become convinced of it. We allow ourselves to feel worthy and say, "If there is Something that loves me, then *I* have the power to love''; and as a result, this idea blossoms forth as a blooming plant without obstruction. We may search, we may look and we may scramble. And people may say petty things and offer destructive criticism that would tear down. But the only way you and I can survive is through understanding and love. The only way a marriage—of employer to employee, of church to its members, of husband to wife—will ever express itself, is in love. Our sole mission is to be happy, sing, dance and to love.

Arrived at a Victorious Attitude
PALM SUNDAY

PALM SUNDAY: I have always considered the journey into Jerusalem by the great Teacher, Jesus, an act of triumph in which he put aside the idea of the crucifixion as such and instead was thinking, ''I have one last lesson to share with them: that we live beyond the grave.'' This is contrary to all what his disciples had thought. So I think that the entry and possession that took place on that day is one that all of us must realize today. Jesus had a great decision to make—something that he must choose rather than something he must give up. And the palm branches that were strewn before him had long been a symbol of victory. They used to strew them before conquering armies as they entered the gates of a city.

We, of course, seek our own triumphal entry and a time of achievement, looking toward being resurrected whole and complete, free from any limitations that may have found us—embarking then upon a new experience of glorious living. So I would like to suggest that your finest hour may not be when you stand on the mountaintop of worldly goods and accomplishment and affluence and influence. The greatest moment may be when you decide to start the climb. Peace within *through a decision*.

When we were younger, as we traveled with our parents we continually annoyed them with questions about when we were going to get there, how much farther it was to where we were going, etc. We couldn't wait to start, and we couldn't wait to arrive. We were older and wiser before we began to enjoy the trip for its own sake. But there in one respect the analogy of the auto trip is invalid. In our travels we can have a perfectly horrible trip and arrive at a marvelous place: we can battle traffic and heat and engine troubles always with the image of that beautiful vacation before us and reach it with all of the drudgery behind us. But in life what we think and feel on our trip is what we find at our destination. Jesus taught this most clearly. If we see only hostility and trouble or lack as we travel, this is what we find at our various stops along the way and at the terminus.

St. John of Chrysostom said that the danger is not that we should fall while fighting but rather that, once fallen, we remain on the ground. Now some of us have retired; others of us may be on the pathway to retirement. We struggle. We fight the vicissitudes of earning our daily bread, looking forward to that day when we can stop struggling and enjoy the fruits of our labor. But I find that many are disappointed in the quality of their retirement because they hadn't known that God's law had all along been registering what they'd been thinking and feeling within.

Not only the quality of our present life, but our future retirement and later experience depends upon the quality of our beliefs *now*. Jesus knew that when he entered the gates of Jerusalem. He knew that what you thought today was what your future became. "The Kingdom of God comes not by observation; neither shall they say, Lo here! or, lo there!" But the Kingdom of God is at hand. Now, some people have said the end justifies the means. But it isn't so in our teaching, for there are no ends—only means; the means and the way. For example, we can cut corners in our dealings. We can be less than truly honest in computing our income taxes, thinking that we will have more, and therefore our future prosperity justifies the "means" (the dishonesty). But we soon find that our means becomes our real ends. To cheat is to be cheated. Dishonesty brings dishonesty. God's law of mind is exacting. It gives to us in return what we have sent forth. They say you can't cheat an honest man. Ernest Holmes said that the moral man is one who regulates his life by the code he has respected.

So enter and possess. There's a line in Mark that says, "Hosanna; Blessed is he that cometh in the name of the Lord." I have read the story of the entry into Jerusalem many, many times. If you read it trying to feel what was in the spirit and thought of this greatest of all individuals, you can detect that Jesus had a definite plan and purpose, or mission, in his triumphant entry. Each of us must likewise have the same definiteness—a belief, a conviction of faith without duality. Now the word *faith* is used mostly in the Old Testament as a verb rather than as a noun, denoting action. In the New Testament it is a mountain-moving word—dynamic life in action.

I have always loved Dr. Ernest Holmes' statement, so consistent with what Jesus taught, that "We prepare to live today, not to die tomorrow." That was Jesus when he entered Jerusalem: not a belief in life but Life itself. He saw, as we must, the God pattern not *behind* life, but at the *center* of it. He knew that the entrance into Jerusalem was a high point in his life—a highway of his belief and his conviction. It wasn't a weakling's gambit. It wasn't passive nor was it static. It was dynamic. Perhaps even a throwback to the Old Testament: move out from the place where you are to a land that I your Lord God will show you.

Now this wasn't the easy way; and our teaching isn't the easy way either. We have the simplest teaching in the world, and yet it is the most difficult because it places the responsibility on each one of us individually. Whoever would draw near to good health, to good understanding, to good in prosperity, friendship and love—the list is interminable—must have a conviction that they exist and enter in and possess them. I've always liked Dr. Holmes' assertion that Jesus was not the great exception but rather his mission was to be the great *example* so that we too could benefit by what he knew by instinct: to live with faith and without fear.

At our Nativity Candlelight and Christmas Day services we celebrate a recognition of the Christ Child. Our definition of that is *an unexpressed potential*. On Palm Sunday we salute and acclaim the Christ Man, *the expressed realization*. The entrance into Jerusalem was symbolic of the entrance upon our spiritual heritage. I find, in reading of Jesus, a loving, compassionate, gentle man of the earth, of the people. Yet he possessed the spiritual discipline of choosing and knowing. And since we're all alike and he was the example, we can all have a greater power over life. That was his ministry and it can be ours. We can erase fear—"Fear not, for I'm always with you." We can prosper—"As you sow, so shall you reap." He taught *all* of this; and I've always thought: if you believed I had a formula, and if I offered it to you for two hundred dollars, you'd probably stand in line to buy it. Yet we offer it to you, as did Jesus, *for nothing*.

The Wayshower entered, took possession and gave us the formula two thousand years ago and proved it would work—but we still don't believe it. We still fight it. How many times in the churches of Truth—in Religious Science and Unity and Christian Science and Divine Science and all the metaphysical organizations—do we hear the words "Love heals anything" tossed off by rote as part of the vast lexicon of metaphysical jargon that we use commonly—?

I remember Dr. Holmes once saying, "How cozy they all are with that!" When will we realize that love is a power that must be *practiced*? Jesus did it with discipline and mental/emotional habit-patterns like those we have often practiced in our Lenten season, fasting from gossip, egotism, self-righteousness, justifying pomposity, self-justification and whatever else we should shed. The whole teaching of the Master in his ministry was the greatest form of love ever: nonresistance. There is no resistance to non-resistance. God willingly, permissively yielded all that He had to all of us without resistance, without any controls or checks. We fall from the grace of that gift when we refuse to accept it. Jesus' whole ministry pointed to this beneficence of God.

Go back a little and try to identify with the mental attitude of Jesus on Palm Sunday. It's very important to understand this, because it prepares us for the whole Easter story. The mere fact that two thousand years ago a great individual released tremendous ideas of spiritual, mental and moral value; the mere fact that he was one day hailed as a king and five days later crucified—all this is history; and unless it does something to make us individually greater it's only of relative importance. This is why it's so important that we get a feeling for the significance of this occasion. It does something for us regardless of our religious background.

Palm Sunday is a symbol of the possibility in us all, of our arrival at a victorious attitude that is indifferent to materiality, to sickness and to physical death. Most of us spend so much time shifting and manipulating. We try to rearrange people, situations, economic policies and government. And after all of that, the situation still isn't changed much. You get rid of one with one face and one set of clothes and you get another one. The face is different, but the actions and even the clothes are the same.

This is why the Master didn't try to teach or preach political or social ideas. Instead he taught a spiritual one. For three years he had been teaching; Mary at the tomb called him Rabboni—her teacher of teachers, rabbi of rabbis. For three years he had been teaching. For three years he'd been telling people that the only important thing was their mental atittude towards life. He'd been giving them idea after idea about what it meant to think rightly, to love greatly and to bless and benefit one's fellow human.

Now, they all said they believed him; but they didn't understand him. They believed intellectually because he spoke it; but I don't really think they believed it emotionally. They believed from a logical standpoint; but they didn't assimilate it. So they said to him, "You're going to leave us; but what about *us*? How are we going to deal with all this—the Romans, Herod, the taxes, the Sanhedrin, the synagogue?" And his answer was so simple: "My Kingdom is not of this world. If it were, then my soldiers would fight." He was triumphant because he had arrived at a victorious attitude where he understood all of this as a kind of passing parade.

Now when he came through Gallilee, sixty-five miles away, to celebrate the Passover, he traveled with his students, his disciples, with his family and his friends—perhaps a hundred. They went around Samaria, crossed the Jordan below Jericho and then walked uphill to Jerusalem a distance of seven miles. And on this journey of several days they repeated again to him: "You're going to die. Why aren't you upset? What is going to become of us without you to lead us? You demonstrated health and supply and food, and abundance." I can just picture them standing there wringing their hands. "He's going to leave and what is going to happen to *us*?"

He said, in effect, that there was a power within them which would take care of all these things when they recognized it. It was better that he go away.

Only then would they learn and gain their own strength. So as they walked up the road to Jerusalem they were singing—just like campers or soldiers on the march. They were singing the hundred twenty-first Psalm as they looked up the long road. They saw the famous seven hills. The words they sang were, "I will lift up mine eyes up unto the hills from whence cometh my help. My help cometh from the Lord."

Now they're up the hill. As they approach the gates, people begin to collect. They'd heard about this man. Their thought is: "If we can get him to accept his political leadership, then the Kingdom of Israel can be reestablished." He was a direct descendant of David. He had the blood that could make him the King. They were dissatisfied with King Herod and they thought, "Wouldn't it be great? That's why he's coming here!"

He decided in his quiet teacherlike way to meet their needs while not betraying his own soul. So he would do what they wanted and not withhold himself from this impromptu occasion. He said, "Over there you will find a colt that no one has ever ridden. If it makes you happy, go get it, and I'll ride it into Jerusalem." But he must have thought to Himself,

"No matter what you or the people here think or want or do, it isn't important." He must have realized that his mind was a part of the Mind of God and nothing could change his faith in this conviction. "I'm victorious and no one can ever again disturb me or dissuade me." So they threw their garments on the colt, then cut down palm branches and strewed them before him as symbolic of a king, a victor, a conqueror. But he had disciplined himself. Jesus was in control of Jesus and his inner Self and the world in which he operated.

Either we control our world or the world controls us. Either we are victorious within ourselves or we are defeated in our own universe. We enter our Jerusalem—we take full possession and dominion of our world—only when we aren't in ruts and mortgaged to unalterable value patterns. We function in freedom as Jesus did only when we have entered and possessed our power to be, to live and to accomplish as he did.

Jesus taught us this lesson: *Recognize, Accept, and then Enter and Possess.*

The Tomb Dissolved
EASTER SUNDAY

Happy Easter! And it *is* a Happy Easter, a joyous one.

I couldn't help but notice, as I came in this morning and walked through the meditation garden, that there was one late-blooming lily. All the others had already bloomed—and *this* one is bright yellow, for the brightness of the day and the Resurrection. It is fitting that we should celebrate Easter in the Spring, and that lily is a reminder, for the Spring is always a symbol of the Resurrection.

All of the things we need to know are revealed on the blackboard of Nature. Nature dies in the winter. The sap stops running. The branches become brittle. The leaves fall off. And then all of a sudden in that hidden death comes the Spring. From that infinite someplace comes the spirit of life and Resurrection. And so it blooms, and the seed is re-seeded and blooms again—an inflowing and outflowing.

Within each one of us the message of Jesus as the triumphant Christ is that there is a Hidden Place. We have that place where we can retreat, die from the world, and then be resurrected with the Life-giving power of God. To me it's the only logical explanation of Spring. Now all of us have been subject to strange contradictions, what we're doing and what we're feeling and what we're creating apparently opposed to what we feel we ought to be doing, feeling, and creating. Our present facts very seldom harmonize with the ideal. Yet Jesus in the triumph of his teaching taught that they could. So today we sense something stirring within us—an ideal that's moving. One man, one individual with the greatest spiritual awareness the world has ever known, envisioned his ideal; and the fact that it was spiritual included the physical as well. The body is but the temple of the Living God. One individual unified his entire being— body, soul, and spirit.

Ernest Holmes, the founder of our teaching,* felt that the death and resurrection of Jesus proved beyond any doubt the existence of an immortal soul.

*(1887–1960), formulator of the Science of Mind philosophy and founder of the Religious Science movement.

So we are here reestablishing ourselves once again in a historical past, and also in a present of fundamental truth: the deliverance of humankind from the bondage of death. But contrary to general belief, Easter is not a passport to another world. It's a quality of *perception* for *this* world.

The great Easter truth that we seek is not, basically, that you and I are going to live after death. The teaching rather is that *we are to be new here and now* by the power of the Resurrection. Thoughtful-minded people say that Easter can't be only a tremendous supernatural miracle two thousand years old, but a "miracle" of *constant* Divine Love coming into focus. However, whether historical or not, the resurrection of the Christ is symbolic of the recurring resurrection and transformation taking place in God's Universe: the animal to the human, the child to the adult, the idol man to the Christ man.

"Whereas in Adam all died, even so in Christ shall all be made to live"—from fear to faith, from indifference to love, from ignorance to enlightenment. So the tomb that we impose upon ourselves is just as tangible and real as the tomb that Jesus was laid to rest in. The tomb of limitation, the tomb of disease, the tomb of unhappiness, the tomb of frustration:

there's seemingly no escape from it because of the great stone that seals the entrance. And the stone represents our fears: fear to trust in a greater and higher power, fear of letting go of the lesser, fear of change, fear of people, and fear of the experience of death. But angels roll away the great stone, and I've always thought that the angels represent your thoughts—thoughts in the affirmative, thoughts in the understanding and conviction of a Life Eternal.

So our personal resurrection, which we celebrate once a year, is a rising from belief in our individual tomb to a concept of rich and courageous living. You and I will never be any more immortal than we are this morning. We are totally immortal. There's one Life, there's one God, and that Life is perfect here and now.

Our concern is not to change life but to change our awareness of that life. And so we have the basic message of our church: your body and the body of your affairs and experiences are but reflections of your spiritual awareness. Your mind and your use of your mind is the creative power of the resurrection from the old thought and old ideas. The vision of the Resurrection story lies not in the extension of life as we know it, but in a continuity of Life that gives us purpose. Therefore we meet together reflecting the lesson of Jesus, who was triumphant, in that we propose not to die but to live. Just as tomorrow is a greater continuation of today, so is the "greater tomorrow." As we live rightly and well today, we are automatically and eternally taking care of the extension of life.

So we roll away the stone. We enter the tomb. We let the light reflect. We surrender the dead idea with a loud rending and tearing of the veil as the grave stands open and the dead walk. The light of restoration touches us, and we are unconquerable and immortal here and now. So you and I need to walk away from the tomb of limitation and disease and strife and anxiety into the light and radiance of the world as we know it should be and *truly is*.

* * *

We unite in a moment of communion, recognizing at this time a great sense of joy and celebration. Something has taken place: a stone has been rolled away and a tomb has been found empty of all our ills and limitations as a great light fills that space within us. The tomb is dissolved and each one of us is awakened to Spring. The breath of Life now flows strongly and magnificently through us all; and in this we are restored, renewed, and revitalized, lifted up into the celestial life.

We accept it.

We know that the spirit of the Christos is now triumphant. We say, Alleluia, Alleluia; thank you, God.

Amen.

Grades, Goals & Graduation
COMMENCEMENT DAY

THERE ARE SO MANY graduations going on all over the country at this time of year that I can't help but think our whole life is class, grade and graduation. I remember George Lamsa* telling me at one time that he had a very strong, reasonable conviction that the Great Teacher, Jesus, went through the Society of Essenes' communal series of education. As you know, the Essenes were a great Judaic society and they set up grade school, high school, college and university in four-year terms. So that after four years you graduated from one commune and then went to another and still another. Dr. Lamsa thought that there might be a reasonable chance that this accounted for Jesus' sixteen "missing years."

Jesus had goals. These goals we find established in Luke: to enter into his ministry, to teach, and to

*Assyrian theologian, Aramaic expert, and Bible translator.

heal. I have always felt that when he finally decided to make his transition, he thought of graduation to a higher awareness. Then I look at our own individual lives. We as children crawl on all fours. We seem to have a goal that we want to walk like our Mommy and Daddy do. So we start; we take two steps forward and one step backward. We fall. Then we start walking on our two feet. We set up goals in our innocent mind, saying, I want to be a pilot, I want to be a fireman or a doctor or policeman or an actress or a baseball player. Who wouldn't want to be a baseball player, with the salaries they get today? I'd like to have some of them in church tithing regularly!

We set up our goals, and we may find those goals aren't suitable for us. So we switch to something else. We may even fail along the way; but we go on and graduate; and at last we graduate into life. They get a job, a home, and so forth. So everything is a goal, a grade and a graduation. In our own tradition, and in the tradition of most spiritual churches that I have any awareness of, there is an invitation to graduate in spiritual understanding when you visit or become a member of any of these spiritual centers. So you go and you begin to learn something. If it seems to be that which fulfills you, you get something out of the teaching, and you graduate a little in understanding. Perhaps your healing work is very effective. In any case, you begin to expand and to graduate.

And so it is that even in our own teaching we graduate. We find out that trained thought is much better than untrained thought. Jesus, the great Wayshower, the great Teacher, taught in that manner. We find that as we train and discipline ourselves in some of the basic tenets and beliefs of the teaching and practice, we graduate to a better life and a better understanding.

Speaking of graduation, I have notes taken from some of the definitions and answers written on examinations by young people in school:

Strategy was defined: "when you don't let the enemy know you're out of ammunition but keep on firing."

Syntax is defined as "all the money collected by the church from sinners." Other gems:

"The general direction of the Alps is straight up."

"The seaport of Athens is Pyorrhea."

"Most of the houses in France are made out of plaster of Paris."

"Manhattan Island was bought from the Indians

for twenty-four dollars and I don't believe you could buy it now for five hundred."

"The climate is hottest next to the Creator."

"The American Revolution was caused by over-charging taxis."

One last one: *Q.* "Why do we not raise silkworms in the United States?" *A.* "We get our silk from Rayon. He is a larger animal and gives more silk."

You see, we stumble ahead in our work because we're after knowledge. We're after understanding. We're after the power that knowledge and wisdom give us, because we're not teaching or preaching anything that is special only to us. It's there for everybody. We try to teach that with the knowledge, you can graduate to using it effectively.

So it's a continuing education. *Trained thought* is always more powerful. And remember: our entire principle of healing, our entire principle of demonstration is based on our thinking. *Thinking makes it so.* Jesus said it's done unto you as you believe. Now we didn't discover this thing. It's always been there. The ancients, such as the Greek philosophers, hinted at it in various ways. Solomon said, "With all thy getting, get understanding." And others: "As you think, so it is done unto you." "As you believe, so it is.'' So there have been those in every age of civilization who have seen these simple truths—truths that enable us to graduate into that desired state of happiness, joy, and abundance—of health mentally, physically, and emotionally.

I can't help but recall this statement made by the French philosopher Blaise Pascal—possibly the first definitive statement in our line of thinking: ''Chance favors the prepared mind.'' The more we study, the more we enlarge, the more we expand the opportunities that come up and are available for us, just as the more one of our children studies, then graduates with a degree, the more opportunities they are going to have to demonstrate that learning. Our teaching is the power of prayer which takes us to the Source. Our teaching believes that it is natural for us to pray —that it is like a muscle: when we use it, it uses us and we accept the action automatically easily and smoothly. We talk about power. There is a great deal of power in that unification of ourselves with the power of prayer and study and the training of our thinking.

What does it give us? Strength, force—and the ability to select wisely. We all select our own good. We also select our misfortunes. We select by the power of choice. And the more we discipline ourselves, the greater we can fulfill our expectations. But if we don't expect anything, we won't get that thirtyfold, sixtyfold, and a hundredfold. Blessed are they that expect nothing, for they are never disappointed!

If you make a decision that you have to live under the law of Moses—an eye for an eye, a tooth for a tooth (and that was the law of the Old Testament before the Great Teacher breathed love into it)—then revenge becomes your good, and you flunk the use of thought; you've failed the grade, and you graduate into revenge. If you choose—and such is the working of what we believe—to live without knowledge and without faith, and to live complaining about health of mind or body, then that becomes your "good"; for that which you possess, possesses you. If you want the luxury of complaining and criticizing, you graduate to the "good" of that in your life—and that becomes your false god.

I can't help but think that each one of us is an island surrounded by what we are thinking. Our lives are more or less *what* we are, *where* we are, and *how* we are. As we graduate to a deeper unity in the Presence of God in all people and in all things, so we demonstrate in our life. I've noticed that when I go visiting people, often I can walk down the street without heeding the numbers of the houses and tell which is the house they live in. For the house resembles them. At Christmas time I can take a pile of Christmas cards and tell, in about 70 percent of cases, who sent them—because Christmas cards always resemble the people who sent them. You'll see some with a little old lace and others with roaring red flames, or whatever. It's all what we have graduated our minds to. I like the fact that, as in the schools and universities of the nation, you're always closer to help than you thought you were with your own understanding. Whatever you believe, whatever you graduated your spiritual self to, is what you'll demonstrate.

I remember a story about a boy waiting on a river dock for a steamboat. (Back in the "good old days" they used to run steamboats up and down the river.) A man standing by said to the boy, "Surely you can't expect a big boat to stop for a little fellow like you."

The boy looked up and said with confidence, "I certainly do. The captain of that boat is my father."

The Captain of *our* boat is our Father.

So we change. We arrive at a point where we develop an increasing awareness of the Christos within us. Then that Something within us salutes that Something in every other one. We start letting go of the temptation to manipulate. Consider what happened when we were younger and tried manipulating people and things. It always came back to haunt us. Always those manipulations didn't serve us well. But now we find that manipulation is not necessary. There is an affirmation that says, "I want only that which is for my good and the ultimate good of all." When we can accept *that*, we have graduated. We're post-grad material and going on!

Take any particular situation (all of us have a situation or an experience). The situation involves people, it involves places, and it involves things. It involves habits. Concerning our habits, for example: we affirm, we declare, and we know that this Intelligence within us knows all It needs to know to work out our guidance. For years I used a benediction for myself and I've suggested it to others for use each day: *Today I'm God-sustained, God-maintained, and God-directed*. As we know this, we're graduating to that desired state of conscious unity with God and with each other.

I think the thing about our teaching that has imposed no dogmas or doctrines or fears or superstition is that we're not bound by yesterday's opinions, we're not bound by our early theological attitudes. We have the freedom to go to school within our own mind and determine if we want to stay in that school, to graduate to a deeper understanding. Our whole life depends on our ability to believe this and to tie up all the loose ends. I have always felt that people who studied the "positive thinking" (and I have never agreed with the term *positive*, because it always implies a negative, and to me there is only one kind of real thinking) have at last the opportunity to graduate in their understanding and tie up the "loose ends."

How many of us have unresolved loose ends dangling around inside that inner room where the mind is worried and fretting on! We now have the opportunity to graduate to the understanding of one Power and one Presence—and that puts it all together. When the time is ripe, that which we've sought is easily and cohesively brought about. That is a graduation.

Now, in our work people who hear us for the first time say, "I don't understand what you people are talking about! You talk about treatment. You talk about prayer. You talk about meditation. What is the difference?'' They are all the same, provided you recognize the omnipresence and omnipotence of God. A treatment is a sort of buzzword we borrowed from Christian Science: we are going to treat ourselves (and give ourselves a treat) by recognizing the spiritual truth of our being. We graduate to the idea that there is one Life, and that Life is God's Life. I am a part of that Life, an extension of It, not separated from It. With that kind of thinking, I am now ready to graduate.

I can remember starting teaching some years ago and thinking that I knew all the answers. After a couple of years I thought that I didn't have to study any further; I knew it all. (I have since found out I don't know much of anything.) The more I know, the less I know. It reminds me of the first time I spoke publicly in New York City. I stood before a group and I gave a magnificent metaphysical talk. Believe me, it was *brilliant*; take my word! I was beaming to myself, and afterwards as I walked out one well-dressed, very dapper gentleman, complete with walking-stick, stepped forward and said, ''Young man, may I have a word with you?'' and I said ''Certainly.''

He said, ''That is one of the finest metaphysical

talks I have ever heard; but in spite of you, I still believe in God.'' So since that time I have made sure that I keep studying and graduating over and over again. When you do this, you're not going backwards; you're graduating to a different pinnacle of understanding, to a higher degree of the expression of Truth.

This is not peculiar to Religious Science. God isn't a Unitarian or a Christian Scientist or a Methodist—which reminds me of the little girl in an old-fashioned Sunday School who finally conceded that Jesus was of Hebraic origin but added, with feeling, ''but God is still a Baptist.'' We often start condemning. We say, ''Those people don't think like us.'' But we can always make dramatic changes in our own self-acceptance by graduating to a position of knowing '' 'I and my Father are one,' and that which I know at this moment touches all. Whatever opinions they may have, I know what I stand for and I honor their right to believe in what they believe in.'' Then we graduate.

I believe it was Sam Foss* who wrote these lines:

*(1858–1911), American editor and humorist.

> Let the howlers howl
> And the growlers growl
> And the scowlers scowl,
> And let the rough gang go it.
> But behind the night
> There is plenty of light
> And the world is all right,
> And I know it.

That's when we've graduated.

We call our prayers scientific, spiritual mind-healing prayers. This indicates to me an action on our part to graduate to a higher plateau of spiritual understanding: not to influence God, but instead to change our feelings so we can demonstrate more of the things that make us happy in our life. Now maybe a few things I have said may inspire you to go out of here and say, "I am going to change my thinking and emotional patterns for a few days!" This isn't really going to accomplish results. It's the stead-fast day-after-day-after-day study and belief that enable you to go on to that higher plateau. *That's* what produced results. Jesus taught it; the great illumined of all the ages taught it—that you can change the quality and structure of your life and your world by changing the quality and structure of your thoughts and beliefs.

All of us have heard the great operettas of Gilbert and Sullivan. Now Gilbert was very tall. He had a tremendous reach, and he found it difficult when playing tennis to keep the ball inside the court. A lot of people would have practiced to shorten their stroke and gain better control over the ball, but not Gilbert. He must have treated, for this is what he came up with: *he lengthened the size of the tennis court.* He graduated to that! We carry the world in our head, the whole astronomy and chemistry of it suspended in a thought.

* * *

At this moment of the realization and recognition of one God—a living, loving God—we have now accepted it in every part of our being, of our mind, and can feel this to the utmost degree. We put aside our body temporarily, put aside the world of people, places, and things. We forget for a moment the floor under our feet and forget any semblance of recognition of the walls or the roof, the business of outside activity. We know that we are immersed in an area of harmony.

As we become still, we feel ourselves attuned to the rhythm of the Universe, the inbreathing and the outbreathing. We feel ourselves attuned to the soaring flight of the bird, to the warmth of the sun, to the rhythm of all nature. And as we feel it, there is a harmony, a vibration of total wholeness. We feel it moving through every part of our bodies, touching every cell, every nerve and fiber of our being. We can feel it moving from one to the other, with the harmony of God and the harmony of all things restoring, re-energizing a re-creation. And as we feel it, we know there is only one God, one Mind, one Intelligence—and we are all part of that One.

We know that as we speak our word, it is known in all parts of the whole; and we speak that word for anyone that may be seeking understanding, a healing—of body, of mind, of emotions, of relationships, of a job. We know that as we have spoken this word for ourselves, we can also speak it knowing that others manifest its creation in their own individual lives. We say it; we believe it; and we accept it. And we say Thank you, God.

Amen.

The Directive Action
FATHERS DAY

FATHERS DAY recognizes the traditional link to our earthly fathers. Yet it reminds us again that all is for naught unless we establish our *complete* identity with *one*—with one Presence, one Father living through us. Fathers Day is historically a North American institution, if you will. But from what I can find, it was initiated by the ancient Greeks, who honored their fathers, and who honored the fathers of the gods as well. They left gifts on the shrines and later they set aside a day when all the fathers could be worshiped. The Chinese people for a long time have celebrated Fathers Day twice a year, Autumn and Spring. At these times they place photographs of their fathers on the graves, and they celebrate their forefathers as well.

Today fathers all over America are being inundated with neckties; shirts; if they still smoke, cigarette-lighters; if they don't, anti-smoking kits—whatever. And the fathers are accepting them and loving it all. Now in some parts of the world, of course, Fathers Day is sort of a complete bust. I seem to recall that there is an island—I think it's called Palo Island—where the woman can have any male executed if he disturbs her contemplation. (You notice it is only the woman!)

Sometimes I think we try to personalize God along the lines of our father's image. A universal idea, yes —but a conviction that there is something more. Father rightly stood for authority in the old days— not domination, but an authority, a guidance, and a direction. Our teaching has as its fundamental principle the recognition of a Universal Father, of whom we are an extension, and it is to this recognition that we turn, using it in our healing, in our work, in the expression of all of our ideas.

Some people have complained that our teaching is too complicated, that there is a lot of intellectualism in it, that there are a lot of things they can't seem to find in conformity with their old traditions. They were told *this is what you can do* and *this is what you can't do*. You went to church on Sunday, you made your appearance, you were recognized, and you came back the following Sunday. But somewhere there was an ache, a yearning for something more.

And I have always felt that any teaching or religion small enough to be completely understood would not be large enough for the needs that you and I have. And we all have needs—vague things moving deep down within us.

What it comes to is that a church is not a *place*. The church is the congregation of all of you and how you feel collectively in your own spiritual awareness. The building is sacred only because it's a place that came out of the ideas of the minds of all of you. It is a place where we pray, but it is *you* who have prayed. The place is the result of it. Always the sanctuary is within; it is the Father within.

So today we set aside a day to honor and to love our earthly fathers. I think that, like anyone else, I was well aware of my father's problems, his inadequacies and his shortcomings. But in our teaching we believe in focusing on the best of what we have, not on the worst of what we don't have. So let's think about the good points—the "victories" of our earthly father. I couldn't help but think this morning that America is full of fathers who were once confused and discontented in their teen years and who are now confused and discontented adults— because that discontent is the search for the Father within and the guidance of that Father. My earthly father? I love him, I bless him, I respect him and I release him.

There are implications that increasingly come to light:

For generations it was believed father was a good provider. We believe in our teaching that there is no limit to the provision of the Universe: "I have meat to eat that you know not of." We have but to accept it.

For years the family traditions and responsibility of the father were fulfilled. In truth, our heavenly Father fulfills all those needs through us.

We more or less took our earthly fathers for granted—it was a "commodity" everyone had and you took it as you got it. But I wonder if too many times we remember our heavenly Father when we come together on Sunday mornings and take him for granted during our week of activity.

We know, understandingly, our father's influence, both direct and indirect. There is that direct "If you don't do as I tell you I'll be waiting for you at the bottom of the steps." And there is the indirect influence, when we're out in the world and we think of his guidance and we're proud of him. The attention and love we got stayed with us, though sometimes it seemed to be withdrawn. The Father within never withdraws it but awaits our understanding.

Now in our teaching there's a very interesting element. We believe that there is One infinite loving Presence that established all creation. We believe, as a result of that idea, that we were expressed as Its life, as an extension of that One Thing. There could be only one God, one Love; and it would seem natural that the creative outlet would be given us to express. So we talk about our own trinity, which is identical with the more organized theological trinity. We say the Father, the Son and the Holy Spirit. The Father is the *directive action* of all of our work. We were given that gift to *choose* blessing, to *choose* cursing, to *choose* our own destiny—without any indication of punishment, because we are taught there is no punishment but a consequence of our wrong thinking.

So we have that marvelous gift enabling us to direct the things that take place in our life. We know that it must come from something great. It requires at least our belief. There's something that says, "I have a mind; I can think. I am aware of others; and yet as I address them, there is no separation. They hear me; I feel what they are thinking.'' If it were otherwise, nobody would hear anybody else. We'd all be on separate planets. And so we have this one unity that Paul spoke of, and this unity is the secret of all healing.

But it's not just enough to speak a word, to select something and put it in motion and say, ''I'm practicing all the techniques and the principles that I've been told about.'' That isn't enough. We need to feel it—to feel it deeply—because the practice of our work is thinking and feeling. We can think, but we need to *feel*. When we've done that, we have set ourselves in position to expose the indwelling light.

There is a Gospel of Thomas that was found by a French archaeologist and therefore is not included among the original gospels of the scriptures. It very carefully brings out: One God and Father of all, who is above all and through all. We are like cells, if you will, of one life. Each one of us is an infinitesimal part. As we accept our identity—not gluing ourselves back to our infinite loving Father, but accepting the Presence and extension of the Father through us, then we worship and become the Son. The Father begets the Son, and the Son understands the Father. In all of this there is no accommodation of fear.

The Father within us is *the* place where there is no fear, where we become somewhat like Daniel. It wasn't that Daniel wasn't afraid of the lions—the lions weren't afraid of Daniel! As we recognize the universality and infinite love of our Father, there can be no fear, for perfect love casts out fear. God is Life, and that is the Life of the Father within us, within us all. That is the common factor that laughs, cries, responds to music regardless of the language but in the same feeling.

And so today I feel this entrance of God into you, into me, as we breathed our first breath of life, for on Fathers Day we get this reminder, as we recognize our earthly fathers, to recognize this Presence too. And the only thing separating us from the Presence is belief. One of the things we have been taught is that we have the freedom to choose whatever we will. Dr. Ernest Holmes said that we are a teaching and practicing order, and that we are Christian and much more. But, he said, sometimes we work so hard at the teaching and trying to be "Christian and more" that we forget the *practice* of the teaching. To me this indicates that we have not exercised enough *authority* in our work. Authority of *choice*, not of domination —that takes away choice.

I shudder when I say *authority* because some people will confuse it with domination. Then call it a new idea, if you will, of authority: not my authority, not your authority, but the authority of the thing that we teach you—so that you can accept that authority and use the tremendous power of the authority of a loving, living God to better your life in every way. There's an old saying I remember: *The only authority is the authority itself and what it does for you; and there is no limit to it.** When in our prayers, in our healing work, we believe with conviction that the authority we use is the authority of a loving, living Father expressing through us, then we have the divine Power manifesting itself to the highest degree.

Now some people have very complimentarily called me intellectual. I remember once when I would have thought that was a great term. But I sometimes think that we focus too much on the intellectual part of our understanding. And the intellectual part *is*

---

*Dr. Bendall had in mind Ernest Holmes' many statements on the question of authority in the Science of Mind philosophy, e.g. "Our whole endeavor rests on demonstration. We have no other authority. We ask for none other. . . . We have to put up or shut up" (*Ideas of Power*, vol. 3 of *The Holmes Papers*, p. 145).—*Ed*.

terrific; look at it: the intellectual part of you chose this teaching. The intellectual part of you chose to get married; it chose to establish a home. It is the intellectual part of you that chose to direct your pathways in whatever form of business or activity you are engaged in. The intellectual part is great. But without the feeling and intuitive sense, sometimes those intellectual thoughts crumble and break.

But whether it's in everyday life or not, when we truly embody— and not in a sanctimonious way, but in a practical, living way—the idea of a loving, living Father within us and recognize that all good comes from this Father, and I and my Father are one, we begin to reach the mystical transcendence that we all sense—a feeling beyond thought and beyond comprehension, something that to me is very precious. You see, from the moment we think even a very simple idea, the idea is telling us that we are a result of the thoughts that we put into action and that they manifest. If I'm unhappy, I focused on unhappiness and made it my god. And I believe that when we unclutter our mind, our spiritual Father within acts upon what we're thinking if we have that deep intuitive sense of feeling in unity—acts upon it and makes it manifest in form.

The process is similar to planting. It seems that almost everybody I know is growing something— roses, orchids, tomatoes; (some are even growing weeds). Like that, whenever you had an idea, you selected a "seed"—something from the intellect that you analyzed, dissected, and "planted," just as you would till the soil, fertilize it, remove the weeds, give it reasonable attention, and then walk away from it and forget about it—and you had a plant. Our work is that simple when we have the conviction and the faith. Seed, dirt and plant.

The American Indian, who has lived close to the soil and close to the "Great Father," has had a prayer that strikes me as especially relevant to Fathers Day:

> O Father, whose voice I hear in the winds and whose breath gives life to all the world, hear me: I am one of your many children. I am small and weak. I need your strength and wisdom. Let me walk in beauty and make my eyes ever behold the red and purple sunset. Make my hands respect the things you have made, my ears sharp to hear your voice. Make me wise so that I may know the things you have taught my people, the lessons you have hidden in every leaf and rock. I seek strength, Father, not to be superior to my brothers but

to be able to fight my greatest enemy, myself. Make me ever ready to come to you with clean hands and straight eyes so that when life fades as the setting sunset, my spirit may come to you without shame.

Our recognition of this can make it a healing awareness, for each one of us can unite in one individuality and one personality: the realness of a living God. And feeling this now and knowing it, we respond to the harmony, to the song of all the universes, to the balance of perfection that is our birthright, to the acceptance of the dominion we have been given. To the choice that lies within our Power. "Choose you therefore God"; and in this choice we feel ourselves lifted up. We feel the movement of this harmony through every cell of our body, through every nerve, through every blood vessel. We feel spouting forth into our individual mind spontaneous, fresh ideas—ideas that bless and heal. We surrender ourselves to the perfect action of God, and we know that "Where Thou art I am, and where I am Thou art."

Freedom to Change Our Belief
THE FOURTH OF JULY

I T'S INTERESTING how we approach a Fourth of
July weekend. We figure we've got that whole
time we can lie around and do nothing. We can go
and watch a fireworks display. Sure, the Declaration
of Independence had a lot to do with it! So we can
watch a reenactment of the American soldiers ver-
sus the British; or a reenactment of the Boston Tea
Party, and so forth.

More interesting to me, and often considered a
weakness of our great nation, is the freedom charac-
teristic of our people—the right to dissent, the right
of free expression, and (what is mistaken for agony
and strife in the populace) the occasional *dis*unity
of our people. But I think our recent sojourn in the
Persian Gulf to liberate a nation that had been ruth-
lessly invaded demonstrated a total harmony. Where
does that strength come from? That strength comes
from the document known as the Declaration of
Independence. And no matter how many courts of

justice alter the interpretation of the law, somehow or other those established rights carry on.

Now we have strength in our teaching because, while we can seem bound to all kinds of circumstances, experiences, effects—even all kinds of despair and all kinds of crises—and while we can suffer our way through these, there all of a sudden comes to realization: we have the right and the freedom to move away from these conditions. Within this framework of strength the key becomes freedom. *Freedom is strength.*

I want to share with you the first sentences of the Declaration of Independence, "dated in Congress July 4th, 1776."

> When in the course of human events it becomes necessary for one people to dissolve the political bands which have connected them with another, and to assume among the powers of the earth the separate and equal station to which the Laws of Nature and of Nature's God entitle them, a decent respect to the opinions of mankind requires that they should declare the causes which impel them to the separation.
>
> We hold these truths to be self-evident, that all men are created equal, that they are endowed by their Creator with certain inalienable rights, that among these are life, liberty, and the pursuit of happiness.

We are born with inalienable rights; and our teaching as established by Dr. Ernest Holmes, in echoing this, is merely an extension of what Jesus taught. You have the right to pray; you have the right to be free. Our teaching says we have those inalienable rights—Life, liberty and the pursuit of happiness. Rightly understood, they can't be taken away. For, once the teaching gets into our minds, we may stray from it, but nobody can take it and its values away from us. We can only *give* those rights away for false purposes, or we can *lose* them through neglect.

The Declaration then goes on to say:

That to secure these rights, governments are instituted among men, deriving their just powers from the consent of the governed, that whenever any form of government becomes destructive of these ends, it is the right of the people to alter or to abolish it, and to institute new government, laying its foundation on such principles, and organizing its powers in such form, as to them shall seem most likely to effect their safety and happiness.

In our teaching, the divine pattern is one of freedom. It was established in the Pentateuch, the first

five books of the Bible, when Moses said, "Choose
ye therefore blessing or cursing, life or death." And
Jesus, the great Wayshower, said, "Choose ye therefore God or mammon." The divine pattern to establish each day for us the way of happiness and joy is
based on our right to choose. So the divine pattern
is one of freedom.

Nowhere can I find, in our teaching, a concept of
God that says, "You shall remain in bondage till I
loosen you." Because we can loosen ourselves just
as soon as we want to be loosened. "Whatsoever you
bind on earth shall be bound in Heaven; whatsoever
you loose on earth shall be loosed in Heaven." So
our birthright is this freedom. We have the right of
choice—to choose our religious persuasion, to
choose our religious beliefs. We even have the right
to disagree with some of those that may be prevalent
among our peers. Now instinctively everyone here
knows this. Everyone feels it. And with that intuitive sense we know that we have the freedom; so that
this inherent nature then looks for a way to express
itself.

The wondrous phrases of the Founders are an
expression of *ideals*, not a description of immediate
goals. I know of no other document of ideals that

has made itself a way of life. Normally someone says that these are our ideals but that we depart from them. Actually, we intuitively strive to fulfill those ideals as a nation. But remember that a nation is made up of individuals. So the nation would not strive in this way unless *the individual* did. In each generation some have scoffed at the Declaration of Independence. Others have paid lip service to it, and still others have been distressed by the seemingly slow and imperfect expression of ideas.

But gradually we begin to see something. We begin to see that this is a document that says *Be who you are and love who you are.* And as long as you stay within the framework of these ideals, we give you the right to live a better life and to enjoy it. The teaching of most so-called Truth churches—Religious Science, Divine Science, Christian Science, Unity and the myriad of many others—is all based on this idea.

The thing about freedom that frightens a lot of us is, "If I make a choice, I could make a mistake; it could be the wrong choice." And yet our strength is *in* our choice. That's where it comes from. So the truths enunciated by the Congress and adopted by it provide the strength for our own—your and my—

declaration of God's freedom. God gave us the freedom to be; God gave us the freedom to choose. God gave us the freedom to laugh, to sing, to dance, and to be happy. But we have to accept the responsibility, as did the first Congress. And each one of us then has the right to choose, to accept, that responsibility.

On this subject I could go on and say so many things and probably have no ending. It's like the boy who surprised his girl by giving her a ring and saying, "Darling, this is a symbol of my love. It has no ending." And she passed it right back to him and said, "This is a symbol of mine. It has no beginning." A ring is sometimes referred to as a symbol of infinity. And infinity itself is often described as a circle, which is why one of Ralph Waldo Emerson's essays is on circles. Everything bends back to us. Think about it: the first circle is the eye; the next is the horizon as you look out upon it; and so on and on and on. It's why to me everything in the Universe moves in circles. Time, light and space bend back upon themselves, because circular movement is the only movement that can be eternal. And this is what we use in our prayer work: it bends back upon itself. We use this freedom to break the bondage of time, which is destructive to us as individuals—which has become welded there because we're fixated upon it. We have made it a tremendous power by inverting the power of freedom. And so in the "circle" we have the right, as we pray, to break that paralysis in the track of time and let the truth of light and space and God and Love bend back upon themselves.

Someone may say, "Why do you talk like this? I don't understand any of it." I remember Ernest Holmes once saying, "George, we *have* to understand these things, because we're metaphysicians. And if we'll stop thinking they're hard, they'll be simple." If everything in the Universe moves in circles—and it does, from the atom to the whole universe—then Jesus was right when he said, "Give and unto you it shall be given." Give the freedom to be happy and it shall be given *you*. Give the freedom to be loved and it shall be given *you*.

I think that this is a subject that each one knows within his or her own heart, and all I can possibly do is open up avenues for you to recognize that you have the freedom and the strength to make peace with yourself in whatever way. Bondage exists in the context of freedom—because we've *chosen* it, mistaking it for its opposite.

Earlier I referred to the right of choice. Jesus said

that you can't serve God and mammon. The Bhaga-vad Gita says that you must do away with pairs of opposites before you can enter bliss. Good and evil, big and little, right and wrong, heaven and hell, God and the devil, I'm right and you're wrong—they all have the bondage of our conscious, finite concepts. But we couldn't have the concepts unless we had the freedom to draw from something deep within us. We know we experience limitations. Yet every limitation we experience, every bondage we submit to pro-claims even more loudly that there is a tremendous freedom that can be redirected if we will reverse it. We may make one thing a reality and say the other is an illusion; but what is really what? Each one of us has to determine the use being made of his or her own freedom.

Now I consider that I have a right, as you do, to choose. I have a right to wholeness however I may decipher it, and so do you. I have a right to happi-ness, as you do. I have a right to abundance, as you do. I have a right to health, as you do; and that right we resist having forced upon us. So just like the in-dependence we celebrate this weekend, these spiritual rights must be pursued, worked for and cherished. If we desire comforts more than freedom, we shall most assuredly lose both.

We practice a teaching. It's a way of life. Ernest Holmes always said that it prepares us to live today, not die tomorrow, because he believed that life was eternal; and as we accepted it, the consciousness of that eternal life would itself forever expand. The teaching encourages us to use the principle of freedom through our techniques of prayer, of spiritual mind treatment, or, if you prefer, affirmative creative thinking—never "positive thinking," because that was a buzzword adopted by Norman Vincent Peale, and to posit a positive implies a negative. We've been taught from the time of Jesus that whatever we think about is done unto us as we believe.

We have the freedom to change our belief and change our life. We have the freedom to look through what appears to be evident facts and see the truth. We have the freedom to recognize that God does not build fences around us—*we* do that *ourselves*, something we really can't afford to do. Our nation's founders set forth in a broad, idealistic way the principles and ideals for the new country. More "locally," if we discipline ourselves and our desires, then we become free and sovereign within the area of ourselves and our desires.

Think of it: maybe all of us, including myself, have chosen a small area of allegiance—and in choosing such a small area, we make ourselves small. Perhaps we even become disliked by others to whom we have no loyalty or love. And in the end, we dislike ourselves for being so small—*and* for being disliked by others. There it is again: everything moving in circles. But if we exercise the freedom to discipline ourselves for the Kingdom of God, we will live for the greatness and nobility of our loyalties and allegiances. It is as simple as that.

The image of our lives as we live them is engraved within us, deep in our subconscious. We can call up any particular incident and view it; we can even do it in technicolor! We can hear the voices. So in essence, the image of all eternity and what went on before us in eternity is engraved upon time—*and we have access to it*. A boundless concept!

The prodigal son, the son that condemned his father, condemned himself and went off into the far country, finally decided "I have the freedom to go back. I don't have to use my freedom to stay here and suffer. I have the freedom to go back because my father is there." And so the father saw him from afar, and a reciprocal action took place: as the son returned to the Kingdom, the Kingdom opened wide its doors.

He knelt down at his father's feet and said, "Father, I've done all these terrible things," and proceeded to list them. His father just smiled and didn't argue; didn't say a word; just listened. He didn't say, "It serves you right; you deserved it!" He might have said, "You sure used your freedom in a strange way!" He might have said, "I haven't seen you in a long time, and I'm happy to see you again using your freedom for your own happiness." Maybe he said, "Come in, let's get you a good bath, get the dirt and grime off you. Then we'll have a party of celebration." And they did.

Let's try a little exercise and stretch the imagination: imagine how you would like to feel. Imagine where you would like to be. Imagine that desired state of wholeness, of health. Imagine that vibration of Love that surrounds you. Now stretch your intellect way out, past those previous experiences that have changed you. And in the golden glow of the day—a day such as this—let the glories of the day fill you. Let them fill you, go through you, and come back to you. Recognize the I Am, that which "I Am" and always will be; and recognize: "As I see this truth of me, freedom of choice puts it into action"—and it's as though the voice were saying,

"This is my beloved son, this is my beloved daughter, of whom I Am justly proud." And so we break the confines of what someone else thinks, and we manifest that spirit of a loving, living God within us. We feel it. We set it in motion. And like the circle, it moves outward and returns to us many times over.

And now in our imagination we feel the embrace of an infinite loving Father—and we embrace everyone else because we feel the infinite loving Father. We feel for a minute that our arms are around our world and all the activities in it. We're not hopelessly crying out in the night. We have the freedom to realize that God sustains and directs us. We feel a blessed peace. We feel a sense of wholeness, and we know that all substance in our life responds to this feeling.

So we dissolve all the bondages into the glory of a new day and we know that that which seemed to give us suffering is now released and surrendered. The light of God touches every part of our being. Feeling this and accepting it, we speak for our loved ones, knowing that the harmony of this moment now touches everyone.

We say, "Thank you, God, that we have the *freedom* to express your strength."

God Expressing through Us
LABOR DAY

R ECENTLY ON MY RADIO program I spoke about
laboring with love. I listened to the broadcast
myself, even read my notes over again—and as I did,
something struck me; something that's so fundamental to our teaching. All of the great philosophers,
the ancient wise and intelligent ones, have spoken
for years concerning the idea that what we think
about is what our lives are. Dr. Ernest Holmes, who
founded our teaching, took the best from all these,
along with the teachings of Jesus, the great Wayshower. And all of them indicate that there is a creative something that works upon our thinking. If we
think destructively, destructive things will happen.
If we think constructively, constructive things will
happen.

Now if we assume that whatever the principle is,
there is a great Creator—and accepting the fact that
we are living, loving expressions of that One Life,

that One God—then it seems only logical that that same creative ability is part of the fundamental urge of our makeup. So in essence we are co-creators. But we can't have a bunch of people sitting around in the Garden of Eden, eating and dancing and basking in the sun. With the creative ability, the highest form of God comes into expression. And in order to create, we work.

Fully eight of the parables of Jesus are about work. We creatively give of ourselves to work. It fulfills us, because the creative urge must be expressed. And so our thinking, our teaching, says that if things need to be moved in a new direction, we sit down and by means of the creative ability within us we create a new atmosphere. So work, instead of being drudgery, is a manifestation of the creative expression of God through us.

So there is a great deal of dignity in work. It makes us feel good, because we are expressing in the highest order the creative ability of God.

For years people have taught pro and con about free collective bargaining. But free collective bargaining is a necessity for the economic freedom of an orderly society. And each one of us benefits from that order. Without organized workers, there would be no collective bargaining—and without an organized Universe, there would be no point in praying. Now the continuous flow of responsible creative action in both work and management is also a necessity. Yet I look at our Labor Day and I find a severe, grim struggle for livelihood. It is still going on in many sections of the country and the world—and in particular in our own area.

There are 9 million unemployed—the highest rate I can ever remember. So there is no room for complacency. I think of the story of the young man who failed at job after job. Finally he got a job at an antique store and the owner said to him, "Now I'm going out. This is a chance for you to prove yourself. I want you to watch things very carefully." When he came back, he found the young man had broken a three-thousand-dollar vase. So he flew into a rage; and when he calmed down a bit, he said, "I'm going to take something out of your salary every week 'till that's paid for!" The kid smiled and said, "Oh, thank you! At last: a steady job!"

You know, some of us regard work as punishment. I often wonder where this came from. Perhaps from the childhood admonition "If you don't do your chores, you'll have to stand in the corner." Or maybe it's the old adage "If you don't work, you don't eat." And there is the notion "I've got to work to prove something." So work becomes a punishment detail. People who don't like their work and who therefore don't create or give of themselves come home at night and say, "Thank God! I'm exhausted!" They are worn out because it's been punishment and they fought it all day long. Statistics show that 80 percent of people are working at things they don't like to do.

Work is a gift. Metaphysically, it's an *effect*—the same as we sit down and pray for (or *treat*, as we call it) to establish the desired people, places, and things in our life. It's the same with work: as we sit down and know that we can give thanks that we have something through which we can express God's creativity, then our work becomes something different.

In the Science of Mind and Religious Science, we use words like *perfection*, sayings like "*Speak your word and it's done,*" and "God *as* my life, *in* my life, *is* my life now." They're all true. And the concept of *perfection now* is valid, if we understand it. If there's no recognition of it, then it seems befuddling.

This Labor Day, we ought to understand that

there is a perfection, a creative Spirit in the Universe —the same creativity that grows a flower, a tree, a plant—the same creativity that lets the great artist paint a picture—the same creativity that lets the great musicians sing or play music—the same creativity that lets the shopkeeper artistically arrange the stock of goods in the small family store. It is all the same degree of creativity.

So to find the spiritual happiness we seek—especially when we think that work takes up one-third of our life—we need to feel that we are expressing God to the highest degree, whatever that work is. But it includes courage; it includes withstanding a lot of grim situations. I remember a quotation from a great general who said: "My center is giving way. My right flank is in retreat. The situation is excellent. I shall now attack." And this is what we have to do.

I might ask: What do you want from life? Do you want to have food? Do you want to have a roof over your head? Do you want to have a car to drive? Do you want to wear nice clothes? Do you want to be reasonably healthy? As we work and labor with love, the result manifests itself in these ideas. Because we always get what we *really* want; we always live what our *real* desires are. But our *real* desires are the same as our real *expectations*. So if your expectation is that work is punishment, that's the way it will be.

Now I want to share something with you about working. This is from the rules and regulations of Wanamaker's Department Store of 1854:

> The store must open at 6:30 and remain open until 9:00 P.M. the year round. The store must be swept, counters, shelves and showcases dusted, lamps trimmed and filled and the chimneys cleaned. Pens made, doors and windows opened and a pail of water and a scuttle of coal must be brought in by each clerk before breakfast. Any employee who is in the habit of smoking Spanish cigars, getting shaved at the Barber Shop, going to dances and other places of amusement will most surely give his employer reason to be suspicious of his integrity and honesty. Men employees are given one evening a week for courting purposes and two if they go to prayer meetings regularly; and after 14 hours of work in the store the leisure time must be spent in reading good literature.

What do you think about that? I am glad we work today and not in 1854!

Work should be fun because we are expressing God's life. Now I have people that come and tell me they're out of work because of computers, robots, machines, and all the technological systems that have replaced people. There does seem to be a revolution going on—a technological revolution, with machines replacing human beings. All of these machines perform with unmatched precision and rapidity. They can detect and correct errors in their own performance and indicate which part is worn or malfunctioning. They can make judgments on the basis of programed instruction. They can remember and then search their memory for data. They can replace people who use both mind and muscle in their work.

So it may appear we're going to have a world in which machines will be doing the work for us. But a machine lacks one thing that we, as a perfect piece of creative machinery, have: we can feel. We can put our arms around each other and say, ''I love you.'' We can feel peace and radiate that peace wherever we go. We can feel harmony and take it into our work. We can say, ''Thank you, God, that I have the right to express myself.'' We can feel it. The machine can't feel it. We can love. The machine cannot love. So there's no way a machine will ever replace us.

The fundamental right of our creative agency is to have an object to worship and not to be rejected. But the creative power can't make you love. It gives you the love, and it says if you're able to love and give it out, love returns to you. So if we love to express ourselves creatively and work at it, there's a great deal of dignity to be had. I remember that a very cynical author—Oscar Wilde—once wrote that there's nothing necessarily dignified about labor at all, and most of it is absolutely degrading; that man is made for something better than digging in the dirt. (Tell that to our children! After all, you clean them up; you put a clean dress or suit on them and you say, "Now stay clean because we're going out to-gether." About a half hour later you come out and where are they? In the dirt, face down digging in it! They want to feel it, smell it, get it all over them.) But there *is* a dignity—because as you work, you express God in every way.

I think we need to recognize that work develops character, personality, self-esteem, self-appreciation; and it gives us the right to receive the reward of the Universe for expressing our God-given talent, whe-ther it's washing dishes or sweeping the floor. I re-member when I went to college in Pennsylvania, I needed extra money to pay for some of my classes and I became what is known in the vernacular as a "Pearl Diver." That means that you dive into a sink full of dirty dishes and pull them out and wipe them and clean them. And they never seemed to end. I hated it for the first couple of weeks until I started giving thanks: "This is the way I can express myself so I can learn something that will bring me a greater sense of joy out of life." So all you have to do is look at me and say, "Look how it developed *his* character!" (Anybody who laughs is excommunicated.)

We've got a right to express, you and I. We have a right to work and to continue to work. Think of all the housewives and mothers who are at home while we are out working. We sometimes think all they do is sit around the house all day and do nothing. I made a list one time of what housewives do when we men are not there, and I decided I was glad to get out and go to work, because they're working harder. But they do it because they express themselves with love. As you work, you express God. As you work, you express life. As you work, you are expressing the creative force that grows the trees, the plants, the flowers—everything a creation of God. And so I think the first step might be to clean up our attitudes, recognizing that we have the right to work and that free collective bargaining is an example of a free America.

I spoke with an employment counselor one time and he said, "You know, there's a job for everybody who wants to work. It may not be what they have been doing but there is a job of some kind. And," he said, "I find that no matter what they do, if they're doing *something*, they're happier, better people." About a dozen years ago in San Francisco they had twelve jobs open for a street-cleaner—someone who wore a white outfit and wielded a big push-broom sweeping up debris in the streets and pulling a wheeled container. The city was fearful that they couldn't get people that were dedicated and cared. This was at a time of nationwide layoffs in employment, and they had twenty-four hundred applicants, some of whom had been making eighty, ninety or a hundred thousand a year at the executive level and had gotten tired sitting around and had wanted to work. So remember if you look askance at the street-cleaner in San Francisco you might be looking at a former corporate vice-president. There's dignity to work. And a person seeks it.

There's a religion to your life; there's a religion to the way you live: you make it your belief. There is a religion in everything that we do—and that religion is "I and My Father are One; I have the pure joy of expressing God creatively." Anger, greed, jealousy, bitterness—all these we need to surrender. Because when I'm working, it's God *in* me *as* me expressing *through* me in the creative talent that was given to me so that I can fulfill myself—without fear, rejection or doubt. I can energize every thought, word, and action with it. I can feel it and believe it.

Now you see that one of the major themes of our teaching is that God can only do *for* us what He can do *through* us. If we were to rightly estimate things and evaluate them—what in them is purely owing to nature and what to labor—we should find ninety-nine parts of a hundred are wholly the acts of nature expressing through us as labor or work. So labor is God expressing through us. And this is the point of the time-worn story you've all heard: "That's a fine garden you and God have!" The reply was, "Yes, but you should have seen it when God had it alone." So there's a need for a new direction in our work experience and a new experience in our belief. We need new thinking, new attitudes, new reactions—to think anew, act anew and express ourselves to the highest and the fullest degree possible.

I jotted down some lines by the immortal poet Kahlil Gibran. He himself was the embodiment of an idea in a way that all people have respected and loved. He wrote this:

> . . . all knowledge is vain save when there is work,
>
> And all work is empty save when there is love;
>
> And when you work with love you bind yourself to yourself, and to one another, and to God.

Yes, there is great dignity in work—as there is in these complementary words of Ernest Holmes:

The Spirit within me makes all things new. Every negative thought or condition is erased from my experience. I am aware of my union with good. I am conscious of my oneness with life. I expect more prosperity, more happiness, more harmony than ever before. I walk in the joy of ever increasing good.

And so it is.

Trick or Treat
HALLOWEEN

TRICK OR TREAT?

Our work is basically trick or treat. We call it cause and effect. If we think rightly, we get the treats. If we think incorrectly, we get the tricks played upon us—because the law always works. There is always an answer. It reminds me of when I moved from Los Angeles to Oregon: I didn't know whether it was going to be a trick or a treat—present company excepted. So I'm also reminded of the story of the man who made his transition, and as he appeared before the Pearly Gates, St. Peter said to him, "You're on my list. But where are you from?"

"California."

"What *city* are you from?"

"Los Angeles."

Peter said, "You can go in—but you won't like it here."

Soon we celebrate Halloween. Holy evening, the night before All Saints Day—when (theoretically)

Jack O'Lanterns go before and light the way into the next world of darkness. I often wondered where Halloween originated, and I found it came from the Druids and their rites, marking the diminishing heat of the summer and the beginning of the winter months. The festival was known as the festival of Shammon, who was the god of Death. He summoned forth all the spirits of the dead, and today we still perpetuate this with headless horsemen and witches and goblins flying all around the place. People would kindle great fires on the hills in Druid country to ward off the evil spirits and the witches and the goblins. Today, we keep a plentiful sack of candy. So on Halloween that clarion call will ring out. The goblins will appear at your door. Are you prepared to ward off their attacks? When that fierce battle cry comes your way—*Trick or Treat!*—be careful.

For us, it's the goblins of the mind we have to be careful of, the chief being panic, because that was the panic that was celebrated at Halloween. It's a time that causes us to look around, see what's going on, and ask ourselves what we are really thinking. For when that goblin of panic appears, the other six goblins will show up also: selfishness, pride, tension, unrest, worry, and above all, limitation.

But then you remember the hundred and twenty-seventh psalm: "Except the Lord build the house, they labor in vain that build it." And so we say when we are united in the recognition of the presence of a Living God, we have a strong house within us, we have a strong house in which we meet together and reaffirm that there are others who believe as we do. The foolish mind will build a house out of the externals, and when the house shifts, the house of faith goes down.

I remember seeing a sign in a church—it wasn't my church, I guarantee you—that said Apathy Is Our Most Serious Problem—and underneath it some loving parishioner had written, "But who cares?" When our philosophy of success is built upon confidence in our own teaching, in our own practice, then, though storms come, the house will remain strong. And so the wise builder builds upon the rock of trust. We say *Trick or Treat*; then do we trust ourselves to get more of the Treats than the Tricks? But if you believe and accept the goblins, then there may be a superstition within you that says "I'm not so sure I believe in God; if I honor the goblins, I've covered my bets."

You and I are here because each one of us dwells in the house of our own belief. Our own lives are what we think and what we feel. Our lives are built out of our thoughts and moods, our attitudes and our reactions. We're here because we wish to establish and maintain that peace, that place of rest where we can receive ultimate refreshment. That's why we're together. We're here to prepare to live each day happily and fully to the highest extent.

But Halloween connotes the old superstitions. Do you believe in the evil eye? Do you believe the black spot of the Bible? Do you believe in the widow's peak? I remember someone once told me that I should find a woman who had a widow's peak* because I would then be lucky for the rest of my life. Well, I never found the widow's peak. Do you believe in lucky horseshoes? I remember the story of a young boy who was walking with his parents along a hillside road and found a horseshoe. He picked it up and waved it wildly, saying, "This is my lucky day!"—and down he fell, down the side of the hill. He ripped his clothes on the cactus. A rock bruised his leg. He fell all the way down and lay there half conscious. His parents ran down and cried, "Are

*V-shaped growth of hair towards the centre of forehead.— *Concise Oxford Dictionary*.

you all right?'' He said, ''This is my lucky day! Look what I found!'' and he held up a four-leaf clover.

Black Friday. Do you believe in Black Friday the thirteenth? Do you believe in any of these? If so, you're superstitious. Superstition is defined as a belief in the existence of something which has not been proved. Here is a true story about superstition-busting:

Many years ago, seamen refused to sail on Friday the thirteenth. The government decided that in order to keep the maritime trade going, they would disprove this superstition. So on a Black Friday the thirteenth, they laid a keel; and it was on Black Friday the thirteenth that they launched the ship. They even named it His Majesty's Ship *Friday*, and on a Black Friday the thirteenth they sent the ship to sea.

They never heard from the ship again.

Every limitation we establish is established as a result of the trick or treating we play with our minds. Now in our work, we talk about treatment. We treat: we pray affirmatively to accept the good into our life, to have that safe haven, to know that no matter what superstition exists, we don't coexist with that superstition—because everything is spiritual.

We all have imperfections. I remember a great man said to me one time, "George, never forget: I have my faults, but being wrong ain't one of them." I won't mention his name . . . but he founded this movement.* So we go to bed sometimes, like I do, and the tricks of the mind, the hobgoblins of the mind, start flying around. The imagination works overtime. We like to feel we're knights in armor or impressive damsels. We are a great hero or heroine being applauded by everyone. We're a great lover (like all the lovers of history). We're a great business success sitting in a huge office issuing orders. And it seems there's no limit to the tricks that the mind cay play trying to uphold our self-image.

For all that, we lose self-esteem every time we don't handle a problem well—and that's why we are here. I don't know what handling a problem well means except to handle a problem so that we are at peace within ourselves, so that we don't have a subconscious desire to reinforce our self-esteem. Lots of times we say, "I am going to handle this problem" and then scatter buckshot all over the place trying to hit it. We don't seem to get anywhere with it, so we

*A reference to Ernest Holmes.

try another way, and it just gets more frustrating all the time. It's like the guide who took a hunter, who hadn't been hunting very long, on an expedition and said, "Now there are a bunch of ducks; just shoot at them." The hunter fired both barrels of his shotgun and yet missed them all. The guide said, "What's the matter? I pointed the gun for you; I put the ducks in front of you. What happened?" The hunter said, "Well, I don't understand either! When all those shotgun pellets left the rifle they were sure aimed in the right direction!"

So we will dream night *and day*. Dreams are good if you can bring them into practicality. But unfortunately—and I had one of those nights—we dream and it leads to insomnia. I was dreaming of hundreds of people beating on the door to get into church. I was dreaming about huge, overflowing collections. I could picture a robed choir with a heavenly organ playing in the background. I could picture the building new and shining. I could even picture a huge office for myself—*so I knew I was dreaming*! That leads to insomnia, and then all kinds of things happen.

Now the hobgoblins of the mind are what you and I are dealing with this morning. Suppose you're upset at a person and you believe that they hurt you. The hardest thing is to remember they can hurt you only if you allow them to. And when you feel you're hurt, you begin to relive and repicture this experience just like a stage director. You're producing it in all of its many aspects—and always so that *you* look good.

So the hobgoblins go away and you're justified and beautifully tall and righteous. If your memory of it doesn't let you down, nevertheless it will distort what you do remember. "What will I say when I see him?" you say to yourself. Then you think of all of the punishments—although our teaching says there is no sin but a mistake, and there is no punishment but a consequence. "Well," a hobgoblin says, "I've got a delightful *consequence*: he can break a leg."

Our teaching is Love—a Love that is of *God*.

That's the treat.

The same Love indwelling all of us—a Love that knows only that we love ourselves because of what we are and what we stand for. And we take other people, to the best of our ability, for what they stand for.

Meanwhile within us the Great Idea begins to develop, and the goblins of the mind do their flitting around—the panics, the headless horsemen, the darkness, the fires on the hill, the eerie screams coming from the graveyard. I remember where in the Bible it says that with a loud rending and tearing, the veil was torn asunder, the graves opened, and the dead walked. And then inside of us we say, "I can't handle all of that. It's a nice idea that Dr. Holmes originated. It's a nice idea that Dr. George talks about. But I can't hack it." And the minute we've said that, we've established it as a fact that we can't do it. We're all basically Don Quixotes tilting at windmills; but at least *he* had a purpose. He believed in what he stood for and willingly harmed no one.

Behind our study of this teaching is the idea that we are, in and of ourselves, a loving, living extension of a Living, Loving God; and therefore we can free ourselves of the stress that the hobgoblins, the imps of our mind, have brought upon us. We are not little, not big; we are who we are—an expression of God: "I and my Father are one." So to the extent that in our work we *treat*, that comes back to us in the form of *treats*.

Your love is a treat; but I can't *get* your love, even if I were to try to. However, I *can* give you *my* love—

and that will come back to me and not return void. Only by an acceptance of a higher Power and Presence, the Presence of God, can we undo the stupidity of allowing the hobgoblins to come in and play their tricks, all so illusionary and hallucinating. Instead of being astute, we say, "Well, that's the way they are." I have taught classes for years, and I have always said when you make this judgment, you're judging terribly. (Of course, it's different when *I* do it, because I'm only "divinely evaluating"!)

You see, *Trick or Treat* says you're a winner every time. If you play tricks on your mind and within your life, you win exactly what you wanted to get. But you *can* have the treatment of Love ever upward ever onward, the treatment of joy and happiness—if this morning you can feel we're here not to play *tricks* but to unite and believe in one thing: that we can be healed in mind and body, restored, and renewed. And as we are united in the *treats* of our teaching, that will take place.

From time immemorial the world has escaped via customs and rituals. From time immemorial we've clung to old habit-patterns, old ideologies, addicted to them by the hobgoblins of our mind. The mistake is not the error of our thinking. The mistake is the implicit denial of a teaching which says *we don't deny what is an evident fact, but we can transcend it by perceiving the perfection that is here now.*

It is important for you to know your own worth, to understand your own capacities for creating things of "treat" and beauty, to comprehend the power within you not only to solve problems, but to open the door to new and exciting ideas. The Power is there; the way lies with you. The *treat* is the victorious living that is yours for the acceptance. Remember the old English saying: "Fear knocked at the door and faith answered; but no one was there."

* * *

Let's unite in a moment of restoring and renewing and give thinks that we can be together as one entity even though each one of us is an individual expression of the Love and Truth and Beauty of God. We are united at this moment as one entity in a collective feeling of harmony and of joy—a beauty, a truth, and a great spiritual penetration from one into the other, with a love that moves from us and embraces everyone. And as we embrace them, it returns to us many times over.

As we think of this, we accept the treats of our treatment. We know we are whole, restored wholly. We know that each one of us is a prosperous, abundant expression of God in every area of our life. We feel it and we know it. And as we do, there is a song—the words by Isaiah: "Sing unto the Lord a new song."

We've sung it; we know we are restored. Thank you, God, for this truth.

Amen.

Essential in the Creative Process
THANKSGIVING

O N THIS OF ALL days, let us unite a moment in that which is common to us all: a communion in prayer in the Presence of God. And as we do, we lay aside the activities of the past week. We open wide the portals of our minds and hearts and surrender any seeming tensions or stress, aggravations of any kind. We know that each one of us is a living channel to receive that of God which lifts us ever higher in our spiritual pathway. As we know this, we can dedicate our time together to that of giving thanks that we *can* be together and share with each other in this feeling of a loving living God.

Thanksgiving, or thanks*living* as I sometimes phrase it, is a time for retrospection. It's a time for gratitude for the fact that we have each other, for the fact that we can pray; and it's a time to appreciate and reevaluate our growth in the past year, to lift our vision and establish a new relation to all the goals that we have. It's a time to express love, a time for consecration and dedication to what you and I have accepted as our beliefs. The gratitude and thanksgiving is absolutely essential in the creative process of thinking, because as you say Thank You *as though you have received*, the demonstration takes place easily and comfortably. But I think it only appropriate on this day to share something with you.

On November 19th, 1863, President Abraham Lincoln delivered a dedicatory address on the Battlefield of Gettysburg, Pennsylvania. I went to college in Meadville, Pennsylvania, and I used to go out and sit on the bench that had the plaque with this address on it in bronze and think about it. Within a week after that date, he led the nation in the first official celebration of Thanksgiving Day as a national holiday. I'm not too sure that this is historically accurate, because Washington had a Thanksgiving Day; but Lincoln declared it officially. He began the modern custom of the November Thursday, and his proclamation is as follows:

The year that is drawing to its close has been filled with the blessings of fruitful fields and healthful skies. To these bounties which are so constantly enjoyed that we are prone to forget the source from which they come, others have been added which are of so extraordinary a nature that they cannot fail to penetrate and soften the heart which is habitually insensible to the ever watchful providence of Almighty God. It has seemed to me fit and proper that they should be solemnly and reverently and gratefully acknowledged as with one heart and one voice by the whole American People. I do therefore, invite my fellow citizens in every part of the United States and also those who are at sea and those who are sojourning in a distant land to set aside and observe the last Thursday of November next as a day of Thanksgiving and Praise to our beneficent Father who dwelleth in the Heaven.

The religious attitude—even religion itself—is not denominational. Religion is belief. There is a religion to the belief in our own personal ways. There is a religion in a marriage. There is a religion in a congregation, a minister or a board all working as one. Because the religious attitude as we know it is a witness to something invisible—a dedication perhaps to the uncompleted, an honoring of faith, a homage to hope and a sacrifice to love. We're here together because it is our conviction that we can build our lives on a religious attitude. To do so is noble and also is very practical. It brings security, joy and satisfaction. But nothing comes easy, and we have to work at it.

So it's good that there is a *teachable* conviction, a *teachable* faith and a *learnable* love. Our church is based on the principles of Religious Science as established by Dr. Ernest Holmes. Our teaching is *The Science of Mind* as written by Dr. Ernest Holmes, and our belief is in God and the Christ of God.

The American nation was built by a religious attitude on a foundation of honor with the stones of courage and the mortar of fellowship. A religious attitude brought the Pilgrims. A religious attitude established the colonies. A religious attitude undergirded the American Revolution; and religion was written into the new nation's foundational documents. So a religious attitude dictated Thanksgiving, and the nation adopted it. To me this idea of Thanksgiving is more than just a turkey (although I'm going to eat my share of it). To me, Thanksgiving is one of the great forces of good in our Nation, the symbol of Spirit, the spirit of Love.

People have told me about being in other countries—how they went and stayed in other countries because they were escaping some sort of inharmony, some sort of injustice, and they had to live in exile, so to speak. As you talk to these people, you understand why strong men have wept when at last they came home to their own particular hills. To some, the invisible side of our nation is like this. I always shout for joy when another step towards the America of our dream is realized. My heart aches, as I'm sure yours does, when we see something done that violates our basic belief—a something that may lay darkness upon our conscience and upon our visions and dreams. But the thing I love in our teaching, in our belief, is that people like us have the ability to keep the dream alive, because we know how to claim truth in the face of appearance. We can pray in the midst of adversity. Our church began praying at the outset of the hostilities leading to the Gulf War. We invited on our radio program every church in this area to establish the prayer for world peace—and I am sure they had already started to pray for it. In the face of all the confusion, we stand for what we are. We're unique and we're proud of it. And we've got to keep the dream alive.

Take the color of it, the richness of the harvest gold: you drive along and you look and see the fields that have been harvested, and you are seeing the gold of God's nature in those fields. You look outside at the time of the change of the season and you note the vivid bright orange, the dappled yellow and still a few touches of green—all blending together for what we call our fall colors.

Take the fragrance of it. Even though it's illegal, sometimes someone burns leaves—the smell of the smoke of burning leaves on a quiet afternoon in November: there's no other fragrance like it. The rich smells on Thursday: the great American treat, turkey roasting along with all the aromas of pumpkin pie and apple cider. (I can taste that pumpkin pie now.)

Take the meaning of it—for today we make a sacrament of Thanksgiving. Think of the things of today, the ever cleaner air, the cool water to drink, the protection of houses and clothes, the comforts of home—for these we make an act of Thanksgiving. Because of seeming turmoil, our thankful spirit today probably needs a wider and deeper expression —a national gratitude unspoiled by the private greed of any one individual or collection of individuals. We are a nation that has plenty—security, peace and freedom—and these were the gifts a loving God gave us. But for some reason, under the marvelous mantle of our democratic process we are a nation of complainers.

We've got a billion acres of farm land; a half-billion acres of forest; a hundred million acres of coal, iron and copper and other minerals; thirty-four million acres of rivers and lakes; one hundred and fifty million acres (believe it or not) of developed oil land; a half-million acres of oil wells (I sometimes wonder why we're so occupied in getting oil from the Middle East); six-and-a-half million farms and one hundred eighty-five million horses, mules, cows and sheep; and this will startle you: a half-billion chickens, turkeys and ducks. (I wonder what the count will be on Friday.) We've got fifty million buildings, factories, schools, libraries and homes; three million miles of surfaced highways and a quarter-million miles of railroad tracks; sixty thousand miles of navigable waters; a million miles of pipelines, a quarter-million miles of power transmission lines. I could go on and on.

Yes, we fail to remember the religious attitude and conviction that this country was based on. The thankful spirit that we have today expresses itself in compassion, which is understanding and not mere sympathy. And we have to be careful in our marvelous process that we don't play into the hands of

those that would destroy us. We have to be generous
—this is part of the great American religious attitude
and the attitude of our church—but not stupid. We
must not turn away those who want to be helped.
That's why national strength is based on gratitude
and thanksgiving. This is the strength of our freedom. The thanks*living* spirit which we're sharing
expresses itself in freedom not watered down by care-
less forgetfulness.

I believe (and I know you share it) in this country,
in America, because I'm free. Because I can choose
my government when I get over my complacency;
because I can speak my mind. I may disagree with
many people, but I hate no one and I covet no one
else's good. I have the right to believe in what I believe in. I have the freedom in this country to believe
in God as I see it and feel it. Then I say, What am
I thankful for? As the Psalmist says, "My cup run-
neth over."

My heart *is* a cup running over. I'm thankful for
every morning when I awaken, and I say, "Good
morning, God; sustain me today." I'm thankful for
all the sounds of life. For the little squirrels running
around our trees, for the sound of the birds, for the
wind—something that is never ending. It almost

makes me feel sometimes like a brother to the Master, a possessor of the Christ, the I Am; and for this I'm thankful. I'm thankful too for the coming of evening; Dr. Holmes taught me to say, ''I sleep in peace and wake in joy.'' I know I sleep in that restful sleep and I awaken to a joyous day full of expectation of everything good.

Try it—and accept with thanksgiving all the good God has for you.

Fanning the Flame of Peace
CHRISTMAS EVE

THIS IS A BEAUTIFUL occasion to me, coming in a beautiful season of the year: Christmas Eve. Christmas Eve is when it all comes together—when we finally end the preparations and enter that great day of celebration and recognition. So today is probably a day of great expectations (perhaps, too, some anxieties about tomorrow). Maybe a day of even a little tiredness because of the many activities of the past week, and perhaps because of some unfinished activities. A day to be glad and a day to be joyous— yet some of us may have occasion to be sad because special memories of Christmases with loved ones are triggered in our awareness. Perhaps Robert Browning's words reflect all of our feelings:

> The year's at the spring
> The day's at the morn;
> Morning's at seven;
> The hillside's dew-pearled;

> The lark's on the wing;
> The snail's on the thorn;
> God's in His heaven—
> All's right with the world!

And that is the feeling: all is right with the world.

Some of us may indeed experience sadness and a feeling of missing something or someone at this time. We wouldn't be human if we didn't. Perhaps the word *bittersweet* says it well. In some people it may lead to hardness and despair. But to those others who celebrate Christmas for what the great Master taught and showed, with love in their heart and a measure of understanding in their head, this bittersweet becomes an ingredient of something very beautiful.

You remember when, in childhood, the days before Christmas seemed to hold a hundred hours each. We began our countdown at Thanksgiving! Especially around the first week in December, the excitement began to build, and it grew and it grew and it grew. That eagerness was fulfilled on Christmas Day with home, with family and Christmas trees— and with the expectancy of *getting* things. (*Giving* seemed to be for later in life.)

I remember thinking, when I went to church as a young man, that the words "It is more blessed to give than to receive" had been invented to increase the collection. I found a lot of avarice in the world. I remember I had a church one time in Reseda that took up a whole square block. At the end of the year I had to give it up because I found myself worshiping money rather than God—money to pay the mortgage. I found myself visiting the wealthiest members of the congregation when they had a cold, but not the poor ones who might be quite sick. It was a valuable lesson. It is well that most of the avarice of the world has been tempered by the greater joy of giving. Giving of ourselves, giving of our love and giving of our understanding—and the watching of the young going through the excitement of Christmas.

But it is also a little sad that many of us have lost the capacity to be excited about something. I've had people say to me, "Oh well, just another Christmas; something for the merchants and for the kids. For us, it's just something we have to go through." But it needn't be so. There are gifts awaiting us—gifts of God that somehow or other we have allowed to remain wrapped, tied up, and put away. These are the very real gifts of the Spirit of God—creativity, love, wisdom, joy, peace—and now, *today*, they are all awaiting our acceptance.

One of the gifts we most need to accept in our hearts and in the hearts of the world today is the gift of peace. We celebrate the birthday of the Prince of Peace. But where is that peace? In how few of those nearly two thousand years have we seen peace demonstrated for any long period of time! And as we look at the news media—where is that peace? How much of it is really manifest? I do not mean peace of, say, the Persian Gulf; rather it's the peace within our own minds—about our country, about the economy, about the violence, about all of the things that go on in our society. *Where is that peace?* Some pessimists claim that we shall never know peace because our basic nature is not peaceful. But in this teaching and practice, we are optimists and we try to know that there comes a day when that peace will be established here on earth. In the mean time all we can do is pray and wait and demonstrate it within ourselves.

At this Christmas Season we are making gifts to each other—an age-old custom: you have something for me, I have something for you; and somebody gives you a tie or a scarf you don't like, so that when you go visiting relatives, you've got something to give them. (I'll bet some of us have observed that practice.) But the biggest gift of all is the one that we have already been given: Divine Incarnation. It seems a shame to me that we try to recognize our gift only at this time of year, whereas it should be every day. Shouldn't the joy of giving, of that awareness of peace, of that gift to us be part of the daily offering that we make to life throughout the whole year?

We have a teaching that is wide open, that is infinite, that has no limitation to it—and yet we make ourselves captive to what the world seems to be following. We limit the offering of the gift; we become suspicious of it as though God were only for Sundays and when we take classes. Every birth is a divine event. The birth of an idea, the birth of a child— every conception emerges from an immaculateness. Every child who is born represents the son or daughter of the eternal One.

So it's wonderful to make our gifts, to send out our Christmas cards, prepare the feast for the celebration of Christmas. We have lot of fun doing these things. But now let's prepare for the celebration of the fanning of the flame of peace within us. To carry love and peace to everyone, to give thought to each other, is the true meaning of Christmas.

But most of us compartmentalize our lives. We lock ourselves up in our own private worlds, only for a brief moment emerging to say, "How are you? Good to see you"; and then we go on about our compartmentalized private living.

I'd like to see us establish within ourselves the Christmas Season in such a way that we feel better, mentally and physically, because, as the great Teacher taught us, God's Universe *has* made the gift. It's up to us to accept it. Helen Hayes, perhaps the first lady of the American theater, a woman small in physical stature but large in spirit and talent, told this story:

> When I was young, my producer told me that were I four inches taller, I could become one of the greatest actresses of my time. I decided to defeat my size, and a string of teachers pulled and stretched 'till I felt I was in a medieval torture chamber. I gained nary an inch, but my posture became military. I became the tallest five-foot woman in the world. My refusal to be limited by my limitations enabled me to play Mary Queen of Scots, one of the tallest queens in history.

Ernest Holmes said that we receive more as we grow more. Every day is the new beginning of our growth; and as we grow, we learn more perfectly to apply the principles which we say we live by. Lured by a sign that said *Antiques*, a young couple stopped at a cottage where two ladies in their golden years ushered them into the living room and served tea. When the couple asked to see the antiques, one of the ladies said hesitantly, "*We're* the antiques!" "We needed friends," the other explained. "How do we make them? That's when we thought of the *Antiques* sign. Only nice people appreciate lovely things. But remember, our sign doesn't say *Antiques for Sale*. We've made so many friendships, we know God isn't angry about our little trick."

Let's begin Christmas *not* caught up in the sadness and the troubles of the world. Let's *not* stifle that joyful feeling of the Christ in us from coming forth. On that first Christmas the world also knew many problems. There were famines; there was violence; there were tax-collectors! There was a country ruled by a foreign nation, and the situation of the people was desperate indeed. But still they were able to reflect feelings of joy. We sing the hymn "Joy to the World, the Lord has come" because greater is the

God within than any condition or situation.

Only through a collective effort can we arrive at that feeling. I may be responsible for my feeling and you for yours, and the peace experienced may be available only through each one of us. But you and I don't have to *build* an awareness of peace. Instead, we *give our consent* in our work to a living Presence within us which is peace. And this living Presence is the Christ spirit in and through us all.

Of Related Interest

GEORGE BENDALL
MENTORS OF NEW THOUGHT SERIES
The Collected Essays of George Bendall

ERNEST HOLMES
THE HOLMES PAPERS SERIES
George Bendall, editor

Vol. 1 The Philosophy of Ernest Holmes
Vol. 2 The Anatomy of Healing Prayer
Vol. 3 Ideas of Power